BECOMING A
Dog Mom

The Ultimate Guide for New Puppy Parents

Proud Dog Mom

Becoming a Dog Mom
The Ultimate Guide for New Puppy Parents

Photography by Proud Dog Mom
Interior design by Alt 19 Creative

Soft Cover: 978-0-9998409-3-1
Ebook: 978-0-9998409-4-8

Published by:
Proud Press Publishing

PP

Contents

Introduction

It's official—you've joined the dog mom club. Welcome! If you ask me, we're a pretty cool pack of people. But, for all the first time dog parents out there, let me break it to you: A lot is going to change. Here are just a few things you can expect:

"I Can't. I Have Plans With My Dog."—You'll start canceling social plans more often because you've made other important arrangements (*like sitting at home on the couch with your pup watching movies*).

"What? No More Memory, Again?!"—You'll constantly run out of space on your smartphone because it's filled with an endless number of dog pics.

"Did I Tell You About My Dog?"—When you're out and about with friends, the conversation will somehow always involve your dog. And you'll undoubtedly whip out your phone to show off those puppy pics.

"It's Called Fashion, Duh!"—Even though you swore you would never wear one, you may one day find yourself walking around—in public—in a fanny pack. *I know, this one is shocking.* But fanny packs are actually a convenient treat and waste bag holder. *Go figure!*

"Oh, Poop!"—Expect to talk about poop. Like, a lot!

"It's Not Gross When the Dog Does It."—You know how when your significant other burps or farts and you think it's really gross? Well, when your dog does it, you'll think it's downright adorable. You'll even laugh and love on your pup after he lets out a little toot-toot.

I could go on, but I think you get the point. Along with all the fun changes coming your way, though, not every second of dog motherhood is diamonds and rosé. As a new puppy parent, you'll face a lot of big decisions and challenges in the upcoming weeks. If little Fido is already running around your house, chances are, some of these thoughts have gone through your head:

- *How the heck do I get this dog to stop peeing all over the house?*
- *Will he ever sleep through the night?*
- *Ouch! Stop biting my fingers!*
- *Darn it…another accident!*
- *To crate or not to crate? That is the question!*
- *What's in your mouth? Drop it!*
- *Why is walking with a leash so hard?*

Yeah, and that's just the tip of the iceberg.

I've raised dogs for decades and know exactly how you feel. Even if you've had a canine roommate before, going back to the puppy phase and starting at square one is always an adventure, to say the least.

When I was in my pre-teens and teens, I had a very active role in raising my family's six poodles. Yup, you read that right. We had six poodles, ranging from toy all the way up to standard. I loved those rambunctious fluffballs! Now, as an adult, I have two canine kids of my own. My world is a little brighter thanks to my Chihuahua, Diego, and my toy poodle, Gigi.

Whatever training, behavior, feeding, or dog life issues you go through, trust me when I say: I've been there and I get it!

Several years ago, I left my television news reporter job to chase my passion for pooches. Working alongside my mom (*AKA bestie*), Donna, we launched our very own website, ProudDogMom.com. It's an online resource for modern pet parents on a mission to live their best life with a dog by their side. Along with behavior, training, and health-related reads, we offer nutritious treat recipes, fun DIY projects, and savvy product finds. Through sharing our many lessons learned and interviewing fellow dog experts, we've gained a lot of knowledge…enough to fill a book (*probably several*)!

Consider *Becoming a Dog Mom* your ultimate dog mom survival guide. As you flip through the pages ahead, you'll find countless tips, tricks, and hacks. I'll help you successfully pet-proof your home, survive the first 24 hours with your new puppy, create a daily schedule to help both you and Fido thrive, master basic commands, gain a clear understanding of first-year veterinary needs, learn how to choose a quality pet food, and so much more. I've broken each category down into bite-sized reads, so you can come and go as you please. It's also pretty easy to jump around to the topics you're most interested in at any given moment.

I hope the information in this book leaves you feeling empowered and confident. You got this!

CHAPTER 1

So, You're Getting a Puppy...

It's happening.

You've thought about it for weeks—maybe even months—and spoken with family and close friends. You've fully considered the time/financial commitment, and made the decision: You're getting a puppy. After searching high and low, you've found *the one*. You know, that one special pooch who gives you all the feels. The one you locked eyes with, held in your arms, and immediately felt drawn to like a magnet. I remember that feeling like it was yesterday.

Before you bring your puppy home and start adjusting to your new life, there are some important tasks to check off your to-do list. So, let's get checking!

THE PERFECT PUPPY NAME

Just like choosing a baby name, deciding what to name your furkid is a big deal. Not only do you need to love their name, but if you have a significant other and kids *(the two-legged kind)* then your entire family needs to agree. For some puppy parents, the naming process is a cinch. But, for others, it's long and daunting. As you scour the internet in search of name inspiration, keep these tips in mind:

Shorter is Better—Aim for a name that's only one or two syllables. Short names are easier for you to say and will get your puppy's attention much quicker.

Yes, You Can Use *Human* Names—Some people feel weird about naming dogs traditional *human* names, claiming it may lead us to treat our pets like humans. But, truly, if you like the name Billy or Molly then you should go with that!

Try to Avoid Names That Sound Like Common Commands—Dogs are smart and typically good at distinguishing their name from other words. But, some experts recommend steering clear of names that sound too similar to common commands, as it may be confusing.

- Joe sounds a lot like *No*
- Kit may think you're asking her to *Sit*
- Ray sounds a lot like *Stay*

Think About Your Other Family Members—Speaking of rhyming, you may also want to consider the other kids and pets in your household. If you have a daughter named Ally then you may not want to name your puppy Sally. Who knows who will come running when you call!

Avoid Super Trendy Names—A lot of people find name inspiration from their favorite movies, television shows, and book characters. While there's nothing wrong with this, just make sure you really like the name. *(I mean, just think back to certain shows. You may love a character one day and feel differently after a few seasons. Just sayin'!)*

The Name Game

TEACHING YOUR PUPPY HIS NAME

Since we're on the subject, let's quickly talk about name training. When you first bring baby Fido home, you'll want to say his/her name a lot!

- To eliminate distractions, start by taking your puppy to a quiet room in your home.
- With your puppy directly in front of you, and a treat in your hand, look at him and say his name. Speak clearly and in a positive tone. As your puppy looks at you, immediately give a success cue *(like an excited "Yes")* and reward him with the treat. Offering praise and a tasty reward while his name is called will help your puppy connect his name with something positive. Repeat this process several times.
- The next step is calling your puppy's name when he isn't focused on you. In that same quiet room, with the praise and treat method mentioned above, get your dog's attention either while you're walking together or he's playing nearby, just one or two feet away. Again, speak clearly and use an excited voice. If he responds, immediately offer praise and a treat. If he doesn't pay attention, you can try this step with your puppy on a leash. Give a very light tug and, once he responds, offer praise and a treat!

Additional tips:

- Once your dog masters his name, try switching up the location. Try another room in your house or backyard.
- Don't overuse your dog's name to the point where it just becomes background noise. Always make sure you have a reason to say it *(i.e. to get his attention)*.
- Keep training sessions short—just a few minutes—and scatter them throughout the day.
- Until you're sure your dog knows his name, don't combine it with any training commands. When working on commands, simply use the cue: Sit, Down, Stay, etc.
- Don't pair your dog's name with anything negative.

PUPPY PROOFING YOUR HOME

Think of your dog as a toddler. Just like a tiny tot, your furkid will put anything and everything in his mouth, and he has no clue how much trouble he can get himself into. So, before your pup arrives, spend an afternoon or two prepping your house, ensuring it's a safe environment for your inquisitive canine companion.

Entire House

Keep Doors Closed—Puppies are little escape artists and wander off to areas they shouldn't. Unless you want potty accidents and your favorite items chewed to pieces, start keeping all doors closed.

Organize Electrical Wires—Lamps, television sets, cable boxes, printers, and chargers—homes are filled with electrical wires that look very appealing to teething puppies. To help avoid unwanted nibbles, keep all wires tucked and organized with a wire sleeve.

Secure Cords on Window Blinds—The cords that raise/lower and open/close window blinds may intrigue your new puppy. To prevent Fido's neck, body, or paws from getting wrapped up in the cords, make sure they're secure and out of reach.

Keep Sharp Objects Out of Reach—To prevent accidental cuts, put away all scissors, letter openers, razors, knives, and tools.

Watch Out for Poisonous House Plants and Flowers—Not all greenery is safe for pets. If you're a plant momma then do a little research to make sure your leafy green babies are safe for your furbaby.

Block the Fireplace—If you have a fireplace, keep lighters out of your puppy's reach. Plus, depending on what type of fireplace you have, you may also want to invest in a shield to block your dog's access.

Kitchen

Keep Food off Counters—If you have a small dog, this isn't really an issue because they can't reach the countertops. But, it's still good to put all food away as soon as you get home from the grocery store. Plus, don't leave leftovers sitting on the table or countertops. While many human foods are safe for Fido, some are toxic. We'll talk more about this in Chapter 9.

Secure Garbage Cans—The kitchen garbage is filled with food scraps that smell very attractive to puppies. To prevent dumpster diving, get a trash bin with a lid.

Keep Cleaning Supplies up High or Secured in Cabinets with Childproof Latches—Cleaning supplies and detergents are toxic to dogs and should be stored in a safe place where Fido can't access them. Ingesting even a small amount of laundry detergent, drain cleaner, window cleaner, granite cleaner, or any other toxic chemical can have life-threatening effects for your puppy. If your puppy has ingested bleach-containing products, soaps, cleansers, or other harsh chemicals, contact your veterinarian or the ASPCA Animal Poison Control Center (*hotline number on page 93*) immediately.

Bathroom

Put Away All Medications—Don't keep medications on bathroom countertops, low tables, nightstands, or any area where your puppy can reach. Instead, make sure they're stored in a closed medicine cabinet or drawer.

Watch for Other Small Bathroom Essentials—Keep toothpaste tubes, toothbrushes, floss, hair clips, facial creams, and any other small bathroom essentials organized in an area where your puppy can't get to them.

Keep Toilet Lids Closed—We've all seen images of dogs dipping their heads into a toilet and taking a little lick of the water. To us, just the thought of slurping toilet water sounds disgusting. *Ew!* But, to your canine cutie, the cool water in the toilet bowl is as refreshing as a luxurious drink at the spa. The biggest danger from Fido drinking out of a clean toilet is the chemicals used to clean the bowl. Commercial cleaning agents contain toxins that can be harmful to your pooch. This includes chemical-laden cleaning wands, disinfectant tablets that turn the water blue, and deodorizers that cling onto the side of the bowl. For this reason, I highly suggest keeping lids closed.

Secure Garbage Cans—Like the kitchen garbage, the bathroom trash bin is also filled with canine treasure. It may sound gross, but dogs love munching on used napkins and feminine hygiene products. Do yourself a favor and get a small bathroom trash can with a lid, or keep it tucked inside a closed cabinet.

Home Office

Organize Electrical Wires—Computers, printers, and chargers … oh my! Like I mentioned above, electrical wires aren't chew toys and need to be tucked away from curious puppies.

Organize Small, Loose Supplies—Keep paper clips, rubber bands, staples, USBs, pens, highlighters, and any other small office supplies neatly organized and out of your dog's reach. These are all items he can fit in his mouth, causing a potential choking risk. Plus, biting into a pen can get pretty messy.

Bedroom & Closet

Put Dirty Clothes in the Hamper—Do you tend to take off your dirty clothes at night, pile them up in the corner, and then crawl into bed? Well, you may want to get into the swing of dropping those dirty clothes in the hamper because, until baby Fido is trained, he may view your favorite apparel as a chew toy. It's not uncommon to find dogs stealing clothes, particularly used socks and underwear. That's because, as embarrassing as it may be, those items are filled with your scent. While your puppy chewing up your dirty laundry may seem a bit annoying to you, it's also dangerous for him. If your puppy swallows an old sock or pair of undies, it could lead to choking and blockage that may require surgery

Put Jewelry Away—Here's another question: When you crawl into bed at night, do you slip off your jewelry and put it on your nightstand? And does it stay there for days? Like anything else that's small and easy to fit into your new puppy's mouth, jewelry can easily become a choking hazard. So, take a few extra minutes to hang your shiny stuff in a jewelry box.

Put Shoes Away—I'd like to take a moment of silence for all the shoes that left our closets too early in life. RIP to the destroyed stilettos, wedges, and slip-ons shoes—you will be missed. Okay, in all seriousness, until your puppy is out of the teething phase and trained not to chew shoes, do yourself a favor and keep your kicks in a closed closet.

Garage/Outdoors

Chemicals—Along with keeping chemical-laden cleaning products in the kitchen, a lot of people leave harsh outdoor chemicals on their garage floor. One of the most dangerous chemicals is antifreeze, which could be deadly if ingested. If you store car and outdoor chemicals in your garage, place them on a tall shelf so your dog can't reach them.

Fertilizers—If you like a well-manicured lawn then you may have bags of fertilizer lying around your garage, shed, or backyard. If Fido gets into these products, it can cause skin irritation, vomiting, and diarrhea. Exposure to industrial, concentrated, or undiluted products pose an even greater risk for poisoning. It's best to keep your pooch away from these products and recently fertilized gardens. You may also want to switch to an organic and pet-friendly option.

Garden Plants, Flowers, and Foods—Along with houseplants, check to make sure your garden beds are Fido-friendly. If you grow plants, flowers, and foods that aren't safe for dogs then make sure to fence off your garden.

Backyard Fencing—If you have an enclosed backyard, double-check fence posts and gates to ensure everything is secure. Make sure there aren't any spots where an unleashed Fido can squeeze through and escape.

Pool Fencing—If your dog sneaks into the backyard unsupervised and gets a little too curious about the pool, a fence could save his life. Not all dogs are natural-born swimmers and comfortable in the water. Exploring puppies can easily fall in and drown. If you already have a pool fence for your two-legged children then great—leave it up. If not, consider getting one.

NEW PUPPY SHOPPING LIST

To quote Regina George from *Mean Girls*: Hop in losers, we're going shopping! But, instead of going to the mall and watching teens around the water fountain act like animals in the jungle, we're driving down to your local puppy mall *(AKA pet store)* to load your cart with dog essentials.

Collar and Harness—Decisions, decisions. Should you get your puppy a collar or a harness? I say both!

I recommend a traditional, adjustable nylon collar as an accessory to hang ID tags. While your puppy's collar shouldn't be too tight, you also don't want it too loose. As a general rule of thumb, you should be able to fit two fingers underneath. Since puppies grow rapidly, keep an eye on the collar's fit and move onto a larger one when needed. If you're opening up your home to a small breed pup then you may have a hard time finding a collar small enough to fit his neck. When my furkids were puppies, I actually had to use cat collars.

You'll also find many people attach their dog's leash to the collar, however, there is a downside: If your puppy pulls on the leash when walking, it will put tension on his neck and could lead to injury. Delicate toy dogs and breeds prone to respiratory problems and tracheal collapse tend to fare better in harnesses.

If you plan to go the harness route for walks, you'll notice there are two primary types. The main difference? The ring placement for where the leash hooks onto.

Back-Clip Harness—The back-clip harness is perhaps the most common. A dog's leash clips to a ring located on the back of the harness, near the neck area, further down on the spine, or both. It's great for small dogs and, as I mentioned a minute ago, decreases pressure on the trachea. The only con? You have less control. For a dog who pulls, the back-clip attachment makes it easy for him to pull you along like you're a wagon behind him. If your pooch needs to learn proper leash manners, you may want to try another option.

Front-Clip Harness (AKA No-Pull Harness)—The front-clip harness puts you in control during walks. The leash is clipped to a ring on the front of the dog's harness, at his chest. If your dog starts tugging and pulling while you're walking, a front-clip attachment won't allow him to continue moving forward. Instead, he'll be redirected and forced to pivot around toward you. It shouldn't take very long to get the message: Pulling isn't going to get him anywhere. Before you know it, you and Fido will have much more enjoyable walks.

Dual-Clip Harness—Let's call this one the best of both worlds since, with a dual-clip, there are clips in the front and the back. This type is commonly used by dog trainers and they often attach both clips at once—the back-clip serves for normal walking and the front-clip allows for immediate control if the dog starts to pull.

Leash—Not all leashes are created equal. While you want something lightweight for a young puppy, also prioritize durability. It needs to withstand puppy teething *(they will chew on their leash in the beginning)* and pulling. Whichever leash you wind up selecting, my biggest piece of advice on this topic is to opt for a standard leash over a retractable one.

When you begin leash training, what's the goal? The answer: For Fido to walk nicely by your side *(not ahead of you)*, without yanking and pulling. Well, when you use a retractable leash, you're basically teaching your pooch the exact opposite. He'll learn that pulling gains him more freedom. But too much freedom isn't always a good thing. With many retractable leashes extending upward of 25 feet, dogs can easily get far enough away from their humans where a situation can quickly turn dangerous.

Waste Bags and Holder—Whether it's in my backyard or on a hike, I'm always armed with poop bags. Over the years, I've tried many different brands and one thing is clear: Always opt for functionality over appearance. There's nothing worse than reaching down to pick up a hot-off-the-press doggy present and the cheap bag breaks. *Yuck!*

ID Tags—Hope for the best, but prepare for the worst. If your dog ever escapes, ID tags *(and an updated microchip)* could help bring him back to you. An ID tag should include the following information:

- Your pet's name ... *duh!*
- Your phone number
- Your city
- Any medical needs, if applicable
- Microchip info or the words "I'm Microchipped"
- A personal message like "I'm Lost. Please Call My Mom. She's Ugly Crying Right Now." is always a nice touch!

You can either order ID tags online or swing by your local pet store and have them engraved in a matter of minutes.

Food and Water Bowls—I recommend using stainless steel or ceramic bowls versus plastic. Plastic dog bowls can scratch and are porous, making it easy for bacteria, algae, and mold to grow and collect. Additionally, if it's within your budget, look into fountain-style water bowls that keep water moving to maintain freshness.

Healthy Food—What you feed your puppy is essential for his future development and overall health. I firmly believe fresh food that's been formulated by a veterinary nutritionist is the best food we can feed our dogs, starting when they're just young puppies. Fresh dog food is filled with quality meats, vegetables, and other ingredients that help our dogs thrive. It benefits their immune system, digestive health, weight, energy level,

and the list goes on. I'll go deeper into this topic in Chapter 9!

Crate—I'm a huge advocate of crate training because it can:

- Get your puppy into a routine
- Help speed up the potty training phase
- Help keep bad habits from forming, like chewing the furniture
- Get your puppy comfortable with alone time, ultimately reducing the risk of developing separation anxiety
- Give your puppy a safe haven during stressful times
- Prepare pets for travel

Flip to Chapter 4, where I share a full crate training and buying guide.

Exercise Pen—Like a crate, an exercise pen serves as a great way to confine your dog in times of need. But, unlike a crate, there is plenty of space for your pup to run around and play. Think of it as a toddler's playpen. You can use a doggy exercise pen indoors or outside *(they're especially great if you want to sit outside with your pup, but you don't have a fenced backyard)*.

Dog Bed—Every dog deserves a comfy bed, but, when you have a young puppy, don't waste your money on the most expensive option. Chances are, your young puppy will claw and bite at his first bed. He may even pee on it. Save the memory foam and nicer beds until your puppy is a bit more mature. Your wallet will thank you!

Black Light—This isn't something you'll find on many *Puppy Essentials* lists. But, if you ask me, a black light is 100% essential for new puppy parents. When you first bring your new puppy home, he won't be potty trained. That means you can expect to find pee on your floor. And, if your puppy runs into another room where you can't see him, he may pee without you realizing it. It's important to find and treat urine spots so your dog doesn't keep smelling and marking over and over. To check for surprise puppy pee-pee accidents that could spark unwanted odors, wait until the evening when it's dark, turn off all interior lights, grab a blacklight, and scan your entire house.

Enzyme-Based Carpet Cleaner—When a dog pees on the carpet, urine soaks down through the bristles and can spread into the padding. So, the spot's size may be larger than you think. If you're not properly cleaning up urine, your dog may continue to have accidents in that same spot. So, make sure to grab an enzyme-based carpet cleaner that will neutralize the smell and eliminate stains.

Puppy Shampoo & Grooming Wipes—Baths aren't the most fun activity for dogs, but it's extremely important to keep them clean. How often your dog needs to take the plunge depends on hair/fur type, lifestyle, and shampoo. Along with a quality dog-formulated shampoo, I also recommend keeping grooming wipes handy. A quick paw wipe after walks around your community will help to keep both your dog and your home clean!

Hair Brush/Comb—Regular hair brushing with either a dog brush or comb will help prevent nasty tangles and mats from forming, spread natural oils throughout the coat, and allow for a flea/tick check.

Medium and long-haired dogs may require daily brushing to prevent mats. Along with a traditional dog brush and metal comb, look into a specific mat-blasting rake.

Short-haired dogs require much less grooming maintenance. If your dog sheds, though, you'll benefit from a de-shedding brush. I run one through my Chihuahua's hair several times a week and notice a huge difference in his coat. It feels better and I find way fewer loose hairs lying around my house. *Win-win!*

Dog Toothbrush & Dog Toothpaste—One big mistake new puppy parents make is ignoring dental health. More than 80% of dogs reportedly suffer from dental disease by the time they're just three years old. Along with stinky breath and mouth pain, bacteria from diseased gums can enter the bloodstream and have devastating effects. It can lead to life-altering health issues, such as heart disease. Daily toothbrushing is one of the best ways to keep your puppy's teeth pearly white. I promise it's not a time-consuming task. Flip to "Your Guide to Doggy Toothbrushing" on page 53 for a doggy toothbrushing tutorial.

Plush Toys and Teething-Friendly Toys—Puppies love to play. Plus, attempting to relieve their sore gums, teething pups will sink their chompers into just about anything. So, make sure to load up on all different types of toys: squeaky plush toys, rope toys, durable KONG toys, and freezable teething toys. When picking out dog toys, remember these tips:

1. **Size matters:** Any small object Fido can fit inside his mouth is a potential choking hazard. So, avoid toys that are too small. On the flip side, avoid extremely oversized toys where your dog can't comfortably pick them up and play. Basically, you're after the Baby Bear of dog toys. Not too small, not too big. Something in the middle that's just right!

2. **Avoid added frills:** Speaking of potential choking hazards, even if a toy is the right size for your furkid, watch out for added strings, fringe, ribbons, plastic eyes, bells, etc. A lot of dogs love to chew and tug on these added frills, causing them to pop off. If your dog accidentally ingests any of these frills, he risks choking and intestinal blockage.

3. **Buy toys made for dogs:** So you walk into the store and see a cute baby or kid's toy that isn't necessarily made for dogs, but you know your canine cutie would adore. As tempting as it is to buy, it's best to stick with toys designed for dogs. Human toys aren't made to withstand all the chewing and pulling, making it easier for a dog to rip apart the seams and get to whatever is inside. Plus, kid's toys may be stuffed with fillers that are dangerous to your dog, like beads.

4. **Know your dog's play style:** When selecting new toys for your pooch, be mindful of his play style and what he can safely handle. My two small dogs are light chewers and practically everything is large compared to their little mouths, so I feel comfortable giving them a wide range of toys. However, my mom's dog—*while small*—is an intense chewer. So, we have to watch what we give her.

5. **Know what your dog toys are made of:** Various tests have found toxins in certain dog toys. So, before you take one to the checkout counter, take a look at the label and opt for toys that are made in the USA, BPA-free, 100% natural rubber, organic cotton, and eco-friendly.

Interactive Puzzle Toys—When it comes to raising a happy and healthy dog, most pet parents know physical exercise is essential. But, did you know mental stimulation is just as important? Some benefits:

- Fires up your puppy's mind
- Activates and heightens all senses
- Improves mood
- Busts boredom *(yes, dogs can get bored too)*
- Tires them out
- Helps to prevent certain behavioral problems

One way to help mentally stimulate your pooch is through enrichment toys and puzzles. There are a variety of dog puzzles on the market. They each require slightly different problem-solving skills and offer various challenge levels. But they all have one thing in common — you hide treats somewhere in the puzzle and your dog has to figure out how to get them out. The top puzzle brands to check out are Outward Hound, Trixie, Planet Dog, and KONG. You can also make your own! Check out my DIY toy tutorials starting on page 137.

CHAPTER 2

Your First Night Together

SURVIVING THE FIRST 24 HOURS

The first 24 hours with a new puppy is an emotional roller-coaster. At first, you'll say: *"OMG, A PUPPY! LOOK HOW CUTE!"* Then, after the first few accidents and a sleepless night, you'll ask yourself: *"What the heck did I just do?"*

While the first night is *ruff*, I promise this period is fleeting. So, look beyond the small hurdles and soak up every minute of puppyhood. Plus, follow these steps to make the experience less stressful.

Schedule Time off Work

Since taking care of a young puppy requires a lot of time and energy, I definitely recommend staying home the first three to five days after his arrival. This will help everyone get acclimated, earn your pup's trust, and strengthen your bond. If taking time off isn't possible, maybe you could swing a few work-from-home days.

Start Potty Training Right Away

As soon as you arrive home with your new puppy, before you head inside, take him to his designated potty area. When he eliminates, celebrate with lots of verbal praise and a treat. It's all about positive reinforcement!

Typically, puppies aren't mature enough to control their bladder or bowels until they're at least four months old. So, if you welcome a two or three-month-old pup into your home, do yourself a favor and take potty breaks every couple of hours. While accidents are bound to happen, it's smart to establish a schedule and start to teach the house rules right away.

Let Him Explore *(While Supervised)*

Once you're inside, let your puppy explore his new home. Let him walk on all the different floor surfaces, sniff around, and take it all in. Praise and reward him when he seems comfortable. Remember to supervise. Your puppy has no idea what's safe and what's trouble, so don't let him out of your sight. If he attempts to chew on furniture or do something you don't like, redirect his attention.

Keep It Low Key

It's tempting to invite all of your friends over to meet baby Fido. I get it. But, it's best to keep the first day low key. Your puppy is still getting to know you and adjusting to his new environment. At this moment, his whole life is turned upside down and he's trying to understand what's happening. Make things as quiet, easy, and safe for him as possible.

Start Using Your Dog's Name Right Away

During the first few days together, you'll want to say your puppy's name a lot. Repeating it is the only way he's going to learn. Use the tips I shared on page 5.

Play, Play, Play

This is the fun part: Spend a lot of time playing with your puppy. Shake and throw his toys and let him chase after them. Not only will your pup have fun and bond with you, but playtime also means he isn't off somewhere getting into trouble. Another plus? He's burning off all that puppy energy. Trust me when I say this: A tired dog = a good dog!

Introduce Your Pup's Collar

Once your puppy has spent some time bonding with you and you're starting to earn his trust, whip out the collar. Before clipping it onto his neck, let him sniff it and explore. Offer treats and praise as

he shows interest. Then, go ahead and clip it on. Since wearing a collar isn't something your puppy is used to, he will probably scratch at it a bit. That's okay, he'll get used to it before you know it.

> **NOTE:** *Always remove your puppy's collar before putting him in the crate. This eliminates any risk of the collar getting caught on something and choking your dog.*

Start Crate Training Right Away

Speaking of the crate, the earlier you introduce young Fido to this key training tool, the better. We'll dive into crate training details on page 29, but your initial goal is to simply fill it with your pup's favorite blanket and some special toys to make it an inviting and fun space. Then, with the door wide open, let your puppy explore.

Let Him Take Naps, but Not Too Close to Bedtime

Once puppies play and exert a lot of energy, they immediately crash. It's actually quite adorable! While naps are great during the day, avoid letting your puppy recharge his internal battery too close to bedtime.

Last Call: Pull Food and Water About Three Hours Before Bed

Once puppies eat and drink, they need to go to the bathroom. While they won't last a full night without eliminating, it's still a good idea to pull food and water a few hours before they drift off into dreamland.

Set Your Alarm for Overnight Potty Breaks

This is brutal — I know. But, it's important to teach your puppy not to eliminate in the crate. So, to avoid accidents and teach him proper potty habits, set your alarm for every three to four hours, and take your pup for a quick walk. When you get inside, don't play. Rather, put him back in the crate and tuck yourself back into bed. Chances are, your puppy will cry for a bit, but it's important to let him cry it out. If you tend to the crying by taking him out of the crate, he'll start associating crying with getting what he wants. Just leave him be, he'll settle eventually.

7 STEPS TO INTRODUCE A NEW PUPPY TO YOUR CURRENT DOG

When I was a little girl, my family and I opened up our home to a Great Dane and a Yorkshire terrier. *They were a fun duo!* Then, during my teen years, we had six poodles—all different ages. Today, I have a Chihuahua and a toy poodle. To put it simply, I've introduced a lot of dogs throughout my life. I've seen introductions go very well and I've also seen them go poorly. A lot of dog parents ask me about expanding their canine family and I always say first impressions matter. Here are my tips for a successful first meeting.

Introduce on Neutral Territory

I've made the mistake of bringing a new dog into my home and starting the introduction process in my living room. BAD IDEA. My current dog became extremely territorial and felt like the new puppy was intruding on his space. This is a normal reaction for many dogs. That's why a proper introduction is done on neutral grounds.

For the first meeting, enlist the help of a spouse, significant other, family member, or friend. You will team up with your current dog and your partner will team up with your new puppy. Meet at a place you don't regularly walk your current dog, but is safe for your unvaccinated puppy (*i.e. a friend's fenced yard*).

Understand Basic Canine Body Language

When introducing dogs, it's important to have a basic understanding of canine body language. Unlike people, dogs don't really hide their feelings. So if you understand what certain behaviors mean, you may be able to prevent a poor first experience and, ultimately, dog fight from breaking out. Some of the most common warning signs a dog is feeling stressed, frightened, or is about to attack include:

- Licking lips
- Exaggerated yawns
- Lowered or tucked tail
- Staring at another dog
- Lowered head
- Erect ears
- Hair on the dog's back standing up
- Showing teeth
- Growling
- Lunging toward another dog

As you enter into neutral territory and get ready to introduce your current adult dog to your new puppy, keep these warning signs in mind. If you notice your pup showing any of these signs, put more space between the dogs.

Introduce Slowly

The whole idea is to introduce the two dogs slowly—some will take longer than others. Start by leashing up both dogs *(if your new puppy isn't leash trained yet, you can simply hold him)* and going for a walk. You and your current dog should be a good distance away from your friend and your new pup. Stay close enough to see each other, but far enough away so the dogs don't feel threatened. This will help the two acclimate to each other's presence. If the dogs aren't showing any negative behaviors, praise them and give them each a treat.

Then, walk closer. Eventually, allow the dogs to sniff each other for a brief moment and then keep walking. If all is going well, walk together *(humans on the inside and dogs on the outside)*. Guided walks like this can ultimately help reduce any tension between the two dogs and help to eliminate fear or anxiety. Keep praising the dogs if they aren't showing any negative behaviors. Eventually, let the dogs walk next to each other.

Drive Home in Separate Cars

Once the dogs are familiar with each other, it's time to head home. Ideally, you'll ride home with your current dog and your partner will drive separately with your new puppy.

Bring the Dogs Home

Once you return home, if you have a fenced backyard, let the two dogs run around together. Instead of fully removing their leashes, simply drop them on the ground. That way, they can run free, but if one of the dogs were to show signs of fear or aggression, you can step in. Watch them closely.

After about 10 minutes, if all is going well, it's time to bring the dogs inside. Some trainers recommend keeping the new dog on a leash as you walk around the house and let him get acclimated. *Since I always brought home young puppies who weren't leash trained yet, I never kept them on a leash for this step.*

Mealtime from Different Bowls

Remember, your first dog has established habits and feels the home is his. Since food is something dogs get extremely territorial over, it's best to feed their meals from two separate bowls. Keep enough distance between the bowls so your first dog doesn't feel threatened. To this day, I still feed my dogs on opposite ends of my kitchen island.

Separate Your Dogs While You're Away

For the first week or two, keep your dogs separated whenever you leave your house. Even if the two seem like they're getting along just fine, it's best to monitor them closely as they're getting to know each other. This is a pretty easy thing to do since you're likely going to keep your puppy in his crate anyway!

I'm completely against the fight it out method, since it simply promotes a poor relationship, allows aggressive behavior, and could leave one dog seriously injured. If a fight breaks out, it's important you're there to step in and break it up safely.

Breaking Up a Dog Fight

Your ultimate goal is to keep an eye on your two dogs and closely monitor their body language so a fight doesn't break out in the first place. But, if your dogs do start fighting, don't try to break it up by hitting or yelling at them. This will likely just boost their adrenaline and make matters worse. It's also important you don't put your hands anywhere near the dogs' faces. You don't want to end up getting bitten. The following methods don't involve you touching either dog. Instead, the goal is just to distract them.

- Place a large board between them
- Place a pillow between them
- Toss a blanket over one of the dogs
- Spray the dogs with water
- Bang two pots together (or make another type of loud, startling noise near them)

Is It Time to Step In?

If distraction doesn't work, you'll need to physically step in to stop the fight.

If there's someone close by to help, one of the safest methods is to approach the dogs from behind, each person will grab onto a dog's rear, and lift their legs in the air *(think of a wheelbarrow)*. Then, quickly pull the dogs away from each other. *If you're by yourself, try this method on the more aggressive dog who started the fight.* Once the dogs are apart, keep them in a wheelbarrow position and walk them around in a few circles. This is an important step for a couple of reasons:

1. Walking the dog in a circle will prevent him from being able to curl his body around and bite you.
2. Walking the dog in a circle will give him time to redirect his mental state and focus on something other than the fight.

CHAPTER 3

A Dog Mom's Secret Weapon for Success

THE POWER OF CONSISTENCY

Here's one of the best tips I can offer new puppy parents: Implement a daily schedule immediately. Because all dogs—*and dog parents*—thrive on consistency.

When developing your daily routine, there are a few things you should take into consideration.

Feeding

Unlike adult dogs who eat twice-daily or once-daily, you'll space out your puppy's calories and nutrients by feeding them three or four times per day. This is a pretty easy schedule to implement since you can coordinate your puppy's meal times to match your breakfast, lunch, mid-afternoon snack, and dinner. Spacing out several smaller meals throughout the day is beneficial for a few reasons:

- Smaller meals are easier for puppies to digest
- More frequent meals help to maintain a stabilized blood sugar, meaning energy levels don't peak and fall so much
- Carefully portioned meals versus free-feeding will help prevent your puppy from overeating

Potty Breaks

This is essential in the potty training phase. Schedule potty breaks first thing in the morning, immediately after eating, after playtime, after naps, and right before bed. Plus, you'll likely take a few walks in between. Since young puppies don't have full control over their bladders, it's best to schedule potty breaks every two to three hours throughout the day.

There are actually apps that let you log your puppy's eating and bathroom habits. Over time, these smart tools use the data you entered to create a custom potty training schedule that's unique to your furbaby. *Pretty cool, huh?!*

Training

The quicker you start teaching your puppy commands and other good habits, the better. Carve out pockets of time throughout the day to work on basic commands, like Look, Sit, Down, Come, Stay, Leave It, and Drop It. These training sessions don't have to be long. In fact, it's best to cap them at about 10 to 15 minutes since young puppies have short attention spans.

Playtime

Puppies have a lot of energy and love to play. Make sure to set aside some time each day to play with your pooch—whether you engage in a gentle game of tug-of-war or toss a toy across the room for fetch.

Socialization

The prime socialization period for a dog is typically between 6 to 14 weeks old. So it's important to expose your puppy to as many sights, sounds, and experiences as possible. Make sure to check out Chapter 7, where I share key socialization tips for puppies who aren't fully vaccinated.

Napping/Sleeping

When you first bring home your new puppy, you may be surprised how quickly they gas out. Puppies get jolts of energy, exert it all pretty quickly, and then get super tired. So how much sleep do young puppies require? Some will sleep as much as 16 to 18 hours a day. Along with planning for a full night of sleep *(fingers crossed)*, schedule in a few naps throughout the day.

SAMPLE SCHEDULE

We all have different job demands, family obligations, and daily to-dos. So, as you read through the sample schedule below, keep in mind this is just a reference guide. Adjust the hours and time slots to fit your unique needs.

6:30 a.m.—Wake up and take your puppy outside for a potty break. Make sure to bring treats and offer a reward within a few seconds of young Fido relieving himself.

7 a.m.—Breakfast time for both you and your puppy.

7:30 a.m.—Young puppies usually need to relieve themselves after just 20 to 30 minutes of eating and/or drinking. So, this is a great time to head outside for another potty break. Again, since you're still in the potty training phase, make sure to bring treats and reward immediately after a tinkle or #2. If possible, spend a little more time outside on this walk to let your puppy sniff around *(great for mental stimulation)* and get his heart rate up *(daily exercise is key)*.

8 a.m.—Put your puppy in the crate for a nap while you head out to work or check off some tasks from your to-do list.

11 a.m.—If you're able to come home from work on your lunch break, great! If not, arrange for a family member, trusted friend, or professional dog sitter to stop by. As soon as your puppy is let out of the crate, take him outside for a potty break. Reminder: Bring treats!

11:10 a.m.—Spend about 15 minutes working with your puppy on basic commands, like Sit, Down, Look, Stay, Come, etc. *Tip: Either break one treat into tiny pieces (to avoid spoiling your pup's lunch appetite) or simply use your puppy's lunch as the training reward! Whether you feed your puppy a fresh food diet or kibble, just offer bite-sized pieces along with praise.*

11:30 a.m.—If you choose not to combine your puppy's afternoon training session with his lunch then offer his meal now!

Noon—Lace up your sneakers, hook up your puppy's leash, and head out for another potty walk.

12:30 p.m. — Back in the crate for another nap.

3:30 p.m. — Let your puppy out of the crate and head out for yet another potty walk.

3:45 p.m. — Playtime! Spend some time sitting on the ground at Fido's level and toss around some of his toys. This is a wonderful way to get him moving, fire up his mind, and enhance your bond. If you have any interactive puzzles made specifically for dogs then whip one out and let your pup play.

4 p.m. — If you're spacing out your puppy's meals to feed four times a day, give his third meal now.

4:30 p.m. — Potty break.

4:45 p.m. — Naptime! By this time, your dog is likely tired from walking, playing, eating, and more walking. So, he'll need some rest.

6 p.m. — Wake up and head outside for a potty break.

6:15 p.m. — Socialization. This could be as simple as sitting on your front porch and watching people and other dogs walk by. Or, you could arrange a puppy playdate with a friend.

7 p.m. — Dinnertime. This is your dog's fourth and final meal of the day. *Remember: Mealtime is the perfect time to work on Sits and Downs!*

7:30 p.m. — Potty break!

7:45 p.m. — Let your dog run around the house *(while supervised)* and enjoy some calm, family bonding time.

8:30 p.m. — Brush your dog's teeth and begin unwinding for the night.

9 p.m. — Last potty break of the night *(well, hopefully)*! If you have a very young puppy, he'll need to go out throughout the night.

9:30 p.m. — Bedtime!

CHAPTER 4

Who's a Good Pup?!

HOW TO CRATE TRAIN YOUR PUPPY (IN 5 SIMPLE STEPS)

Before you even bring baby Fido home, do yourself a favor and get a crate. If you've never raised a puppy before then the idea of putting your canine companion in a cage may seem a bit cruel, as if you're locking him up in a jail cell. I thought the same thing back in the day. But, when used correctly, your puppy will actually enjoy the crate and it will help him thrive.

Crates offer a safe and controlled setting, which is especially helpful when your curious puppy can't have your full attention. And get this: Since dogs are naturally den animals, they actually like confined spaces. The crate can quickly become a secure place for your pooch to rest and relax. A few benefits of crate training your dog:

- Gets your puppy into a routine
- Helps speed up the potty training phase
- Helps keep bad habits from forming, like chewing the furniture
- Gets your puppy comfortable with alone time, ultimately reducing the risk of developing separation anxiety
- Gives your puppy a safe haven during stressful times
- Prepares pets for travel

Step 1: Fill the Crate With Your Pup's Stuff

Before introducing your puppy to the crate, fill it up with his bed or blanket and some special toys. This will help him view the crate as a warm, welcoming, and fun space.

Step 2: Introduce Your Dog to the Crate With an Open Door

Once the crate is all set up, let your pup explore! If he sniffs around and shows interest on his own, give lots of praise. If not, sit on the ground next to the crate and, with a happy tone to your voice, call your canine kid over.

After he spends some time investigating and playing near the crate, invite your pup inside. Never force your puppy inside, as this will create a negative experience. Instead, you want him to go inside on his own. To make a walk inside more appealing, put a high-value treat (*like a piece of boiled chicken, dehydrated liver bites, or a sardine-based treat*) in the middle of the crate. Once your puppy walks inside, it's time to praise, praise, praise. You always want to make the crate a positive place, so praise is super important.

Another great way you can encourage your puppy to walk inside the crate is to place his food bowl in there during mealtimes. Again, it's essential to keep the door open while your puppy gets used to the crate, as you don't want him to feel trapped.

Step 3: Close the Door for a Short Time

Once your puppy seems comfortable inside the crate and is walking in there on his own, it's time to close the door. At first, only keep the door shut for a few seconds, so your puppy doesn't even have time to react. When you open the door, give lots of praise. Repeat this step several times, keeping the door closed for a slightly longer period each time.

To make this step even more comfortable for your pup, you can leave a yummy treat-filled KONG inside.

Take your time with this step. In the beginning, you don't want your pup to associate a closed door with you leaving (*because that can be scary for your pup*). So, just sit down and hang out near the crate and practice opening and closing the door, until

your pooch seems relaxed. Ideally, you'll practice this step several times throughout the day.

Step 4: Leave the Room

Now that your puppy is familiar with the crate and isn't afraid of a closed door, try leaving the room. Leave your puppy in the crate for about a minute or two. Again, to make this step easier on your puppy, you can leave a treat-filled KONG inside the crate.

When you come back into the room, stay calm. If your pet is whining, wait to open the door until he calms down. If you let your little one out when he cries, he will associate crying with getting what he wants.

Step 5: Leave the House

The first few times you leave your dog home alone in the crate, only leave for a short time. Try a quick trip to the gas station or grocery store. *Note: When leaving the house, don't leave a treat-filled KONG inside the crate. It's better to supervise your dog during this type of play.*

Extra Tips

- Don't rush the process. While some dogs take to the crate right away, it may take others longer.
- Never use the crate as a form of punishment. The crate should always be viewed as a positive place and somewhere your furbaby can go to feel safe.
- Don't leave your puppy in the crate for prolonged periods, to avoid soiling inside their den. Cap crate time at four hours.
- Put your puppy's crate in an area where your family spends a lot of time. Don't put it in an isolated section of your home or, worse, outside.
- Remove your puppy's collar before leaving him in the crate. This eliminates any risk of the collar getting caught on something and choking your dog.

- Check the temperature around your puppy's crate to ensure it's not too hot or too cold. You want to make your puppy as comfortable as possible.

- Make sure nothing is hanging or dangling into the crate that could potentially harm your puppy.

Choosing the Right Crate for Your Dog

Brands, types, and sizes—there are a bunch of different crates on the market, and picking the right one is essential.

One of the biggest mistakes dog owners make when choosing a crate is getting one that's way too big. If you're using the crate to help with potty training, an oversized crate will defeat the purpose. It should be large enough for your puppy to stand up, turn around, and stretch. But it shouldn't be so large that they can go to the bathroom on one end and sleep on the other end. By nature, dogs don't want to soil where they eat and sleep.

Now let's talk about types of crates:

Wire Crate—This is the most popular crate type and ideal for the average puppy. It comes with a removable plastic tray for easy clean-up and most are collapsible, making them great for travel. The only drawbacks: They aren't very aesthetically pleasing and, if your dog is a little Houdini, he may figure out how to open up the lock and escape.

Plastic Crate—This type of crate is great for escape artists, however, be mindful of ventilation. Some (not all) plastic crates feature fewer openings, meaning the air circulation isn't always the best.

Soft-Sided Crate—While this type of crate is more aesthetically pleasing than wire or plastic crates, it's not ideal for all dogs. Since soft-sided crates are typically made of canvas and mesh, destructive dogs can do a number on the walls. So, if your dog likes to scratch and chew at his crate, don't opt for this type.

Decorative Furniture Crate—This type of crate is typically made out of wood and can double as an end table. While it's definitely the most aesthetically pleasing, they aren't ideal for young puppies in the training phase. That's because they aren't as easy to clean, they're not portable, and teething puppies may puncture holes into the wood. Plus, the other drawback is the price tag!

7 POTTY TRAINING TIPS

Knee deep in urine and feces…ohhhh the joy of being a dog mom!

When you first welcome baby Fido into your home, he'll have no idea where he's allowed—or not allowed—to *go*. So, when he feels the urge to pee or poo, he won't know to run over to the door and ask to go outside. Realistically, he'll just let it rip right there on the floor, couch, bed, or wherever he is at the moment. Or, if your puppy is standing on your lap then he may just tinkle on you *(let this serve as your official heads up—it happens)*!

You also shouldn't expect baby Fido to settle into his new home and immediately understand the concept of *holding it*. Puppies don't have fully developed bladder muscles until they're at least four to six months old. So, potty training is a process.

Throughout this process, it's important to remember your pooch doesn't want to be a dirty dog. You just need to be patient and teach him what to do.

Don't Turn to Pee Pads

I know some people will disagree with me on this. And I get it. Pee pads are beneficial at times. They're great for unvaccinated puppies living in busy apartment complexes, small breeds during harsh winter months, and elderly/disabled pooches who have trouble walking. However, for the average dog mom, I'm not a believer in training pee pads. Think about it—pee pads teach your furbaby it's *okay* to go to the bathroom in the house. That's the total opposite of what you are trying to teach him. So, unless you plan to use pee pads for the rest of your dog's life *(and some people may)* then they're simply adding an extra step to the training process.

The Crate is Your Best Friend

Crates offer a lot of benefits, and speeding up the potty training process is just one of them. Using the crate whenever you can't keep an eye on Fido will help cut back on accidents around the house. The fewer accidents, the better.

Have a Set Schedule

As highlighted in Chapter 3, the key to success is consistency. Once your puppy starts to understand his potty is outside and you bring him to his potty every time he wakes up, shortly after he eats, and before he goes in his crate, he'll quickly adapt to the pattern.

Go for Frequent Walks

Remember: Young puppies aren't mature enough to control their bladder or bowels. For some, it may take four months. For others, it may even take up to six months. So, until your puppy is fully trained, go for walks every couple of hours and stick with your strict schedule.

Watch for Signs

Does your dog look distracted? Is he sniffing the rug, pacing, and whining? These are all signs your puppy needs to go to the bathroom. If you notice this behavior, ask your puppy if he wants to go out and then immediately take a potty break.

Positive Reinforcement

Treats and praise go a long way. If you celebrate your dog's success when he does something right, he'll keep doing it. Always remember: Your dog wants to make you happy. You just need to show him how to do that.

Don't Punish

You never want your dog to associate the going action with negativity. If you catch your dog in the act, don't scream at him. Instead, get his attention by clapping your hands loudly. This will alert him that he's doing something wrong. Then bring him outside. Once he's finished doing his business, give him a treat and praise.

If you discover an accident on your floor but didn't catch your dog in the act, simply clean it up and try keeping a closer eye on him next time. Don't get angry or rub your dog's nose in it. Puppies aren't able to connect your anger with their earlier accident.

How to Wean Your Puppy Off Pee Pads

If your furbaby is already trained to pee pads when you bring him home, and you intend on moving his potty to the backyard, your job is to re-train.

At first, your puppy isn't going to understand why you're moving his bathroom from the pee pad to outside. Think of it from his point of view. When your pooch is used to going on a pee pad in the house, he never has to exert any real control. He gets the urge to go, walks over to the pad, and relieves himself. So now, not only do you want to change where he goes, but you also want him to hold his urges until you get him there.

For you: "Yay, no more pee pads."

For him: "What the heck?!"

You can't just take the pee pad away or else your furbaby will likely just run to that same spot and tinkle on the floor. With that in mind, the pee pad will become your best training tool.

Step 1: Move the Pad Closer to the Door

The goal here is to move your dog's potty closer to the outside. Don't rush this process. You're going to have to move the pad slowly until you get to the door. This process could take up to two weeks, depending on where you usually keep the pee pad. If you try to move it too quickly, you increase the chance of accidents.

Another tip: Every time you move your puppy's pad, let him watch. Then, once your puppy uses the pad in its new spot, offer lots of praise. As I've mentioned, praise works wonders because your furbaby thrives when he pleases you.

Step 2: Move Your Dog Outside

Once the pee pad is right near the door, the next step is to finally move outside. Whenever you see your puppy run over to the pee pad to relieve himself, quickly grab his leash and ask if he wants to go *Out*. Then, bring him outside to do his business. For some dogs, it also helps to bring the pee pad outside. Before you know it, your puppy should be going over to the door and asking to go out.

Disinfect

When you move the pee pad, thoroughly disinfect the floor. This is very important since you don't want to leave any scents behind to attract your dog. You'll want to use a bio-enzymatic formula to break down and permanently destroy urine and fecal odors. There are many brands available at your local pet store. Flip to page 148 for more on this topic!

Remove Throw Rugs and Floor Mats

If you have throw rugs around your house or floor mats by your doors, remove them during the training period. At this time, your pooch may see these rugs as replacement pads and go on them. I say this from experience because I had a dog who did this. I removed the throw rug and she was fine. After she acclimated to her outdoor potty, I was able to return the rug.

Stop Excited Wee-ers From Weeing

Since we're on the topic of urine, let's talk about excited peeing. A lot of puppies pee when they feel overjoyed. It usually happens when they first see someone or during playtime. While most puppies grow out of this, there is something you can do to help curb unwanted pee on the floor.

Keep Greetings Low-Key
(I Mean Really Low-Key)

Baby talk, kisses, and big hugs... are you guilty of riling up your easily-excited dog when you first get home? Since excited urination typically happens during greetings, try to keep them as low-key as possible.

Here's the routine that worked for me: After you walk into your home, ignore your puppy. I know how it sounds, but trust me. Since petting and eye contact are enough to get some wee-ers squirting, when you first walk through your door, just walk past your puppy, grab his leash, calmly hook it up to his harness, and head outside. Once your puppy has gone to the bathroom, give lots of praise.

Ask Your Friends/Family to Do the Same

When you're having company over, walk your puppy right before they arrive. Then, as they come inside, ask your friends and family members to ignore Fido until he settles down. After a few minutes, let them gently pet your pup. Make sure the delayed greeting is still low-key and calm.

Don't Punish

While excited peeing may be annoying, don't punish your dog for it. He doesn't understand. He isn't peeing in the house because he's not house-trained. He's simply unable to control himself.

WHY YOU SHOULDN'T TELL YOUR PUPPY "NO" (ALL THE TIME)

Before we dive into basic commands and early training tips, let me ask you a question: When your puppy does something undesirable, what's your first reaction? A lot of people immediately sternly shout, "No!" And if their canine kid doesn't listen the first time, they may say it again … only this time louder and longer. *"NOOOO!"* Now let me ask you another question: Do you really think your dog didn't hear you the first time?

Dogs have exceptional hearing—much better than ours. Repeatedly shouting the same command over and over isn't going to get your dog to listen. Rather, it's only going to cause your dog stress and confusion. Because, at the end of the day, your dog may not actually understand what the word *No* really means.

The Problems With *No* When Used for Every Unwanted Action

When your dog barks excessively, jumps on guests, chews up shoes, and digs holes in your perfectly manicured yard, it's important to remember he's only doing what comes naturally to him. He doesn't know he's doing something *wrong*. To modify your pup's unwanted behavior, you have to teach him what you want him to do instead.

The two big problems with the word *No*:

1. It doesn't teach your dog what he should do. If your dog jumps on people when they walk through the door, for example, it's much more effective to instruct your dog to Sit.

By constantly redirecting your dog's behavior—versus negatively telling him what not to do—he will eventually learn good habits.

2. It's a rather ambiguous command. Say your dog is on the couch eating some stolen food scraps. If you yell, "No!" then how does your dog know exactly what he's doing wrong? Was it bad to hang out on the couch or eat the leftover food scraps?

A Better Method

Rather than saying *no* to everything and focusing on the action you don't want your dog doing, switch your focus to what you do want your dog doing. Then, clearly redirect and teach good behavior. Here are a few examples:

- If you catch your dog chewing one of your shoes then tell him to *Drop It* and redirect him to play with an appropriate toy instead
- If you find your dog sniffing something he shouldn't eat then tell him to *Leave It*
- If your dog is barking excessively then tell him *Quiet*
- If you don't want your dog on the couch then tell him *Off*
- If your dog tugs on the leash during walks then simply stop walking and teach the word *Heel*

See the difference?

What is Clicker Training?

We're about to dive into basic command training. But, before we do, let's quickly chat about clickers. Clicker training is a type of positive reinforcement that lets you quickly and effectively tell your dog when they performed a desirable action. When used correctly, the clicker can help speed up the training process. Here's how it works:

1. Your dog does something desirable.
2. That exact moment, you mark the good behavior with the clicker. (*A clicker is a small, inexpensive, handheld device that features a metal strip inside. Once you press the clicker's button, it makes a distinctive click sound.*)
3. Once you click the clicker, immediately reinforce the good behavior with a treat. The timing of the click and the subsequent treat is essential.

Many trainers recommend the clicker because it's much faster and more distinct than solely saying "good boy" or "good girl." Unlike our voices, which can differ depending on our mood, the clicker's delivery is always the same. Plus, the click sound produced by this noisemaker is unique—one your dog only hears while training.

Before you begin using the clicker for commands, spend some time teaching your dog what the click sound means. So, in a quiet room with no distraction, sit in front of your dog. Once he's sitting calmly, click the clicker and immediately follow it up with a tasty treat and praise. (*Since the clicker's sound can be startling to a dog at first, try muffling it a bit with your hand.*) Do this several times, so your dog begins associating the sound with the reward. Throughout the day, when your dog does something desirable, click the clicker and immediately follow it up with a treat. Your dog will quickly associate good behavior with a click, and a click with something yummy. Of course, while clicker training, don't forget to still praise your puppy. Attention and affection go a long way.

As you read through the next few pages, you'll notice I don't always mention the clicker. But, if you do plan to use a clicker in your training sessions, keep the above tips in mind!

ESSENTIAL COMMANDS EVERY PUPPY SHOULD KNOW

Sit

This is usually the first command people teach their young puppies. While it seems pretty basic, it's actually very important for young Fido to master. Sit can help settle down your dog when needed. Plus, it plays an important role in managing unwanted behaviors, as a dog can't jump on people, steal food from the table, or chase after something while sitting.

- Start by holding a training treat close to your dog's nose. Once he gets a good whiff and shows interest in the treat, slowly move your treat-filled hand upward. Your dog's snout should stay glued to your hand, as if the two are magnets. By raising your hand, this should cause your dog to tilt his head up and his bottom should lower to the ground. Once your pup's booty touches the ground (not just hovering, but actually touching), immediately give a reward marker (either click the clicker or say a verbal marker, like "Yes!" in an upbeat tone) and offer the treat. Follow up the treat with praise and petting. Keep in mind: You shouldn't need to press your dog's tush to the floor. Let it come naturally. Repeat this process several times, until your dog begins sitting at the sight of the treat moving above his nose.
- Once your dog gets the hang of things, add in the cue word. While holding the treat, say the word "Sit" as you begin lifting your hand. Again, once your dog's bottom touches the ground, give the reward marker, treat, and praise.

- The next step is to repeat the same process with an empty hand. As you cue your dog to Sit, I recommend pinching your fingers together (as if you're holding a treat) and doing a similar hand motion (like a scooping-up action). Once your dog's bottom hits the ground, give the reward marker and offer a treat (one you were hiding in your other hand).
- Once your dog is mastering the Sit command in a quiet room, change up the location. Practice in other rooms and eventually outdoors. This will naturally increase the number of distractions present, but that's a good thing. Ultimately, you want your dog to listen to your Sit command despite his surroundings.

Down

Once your dog masters the Sit command, it's time to take things to the next level and teach the Down command. Similar to Sit, this command can help manage unwanted behaviors. It also promotes relaxation and calmness in hyper dogs.

- With a treat in your hand, first, direct your dog to Sit.
- Beginning with the treat directly in front of your dog's nose, slowly lower your hand to the floor. This should prompt your dog to lower down to the ground. As soon as your dog's elbows touch the floor and he enters the Down position, immediately give a reward marker (either click the clicker or say a verbal marker, like "Yes!" in an upbeat

tone) and offer the treat. Follow up the treat with praise and petting. Keep in mind: You shouldn't need to press your dog's body down to the floor. Let it come naturally. Repeat this process several times, until your dog begins lying down at the sight of the treat moving toward the ground.

- Once your dog gets the hang of things, add in the cue word. Once your dog is sitting and you're holding the treat in front of him, say the word "Lie Down" or just "Down" and begin lowering your hand. Again, once your dog is fully lying on the ground, give the reward marker, treat, and praise.
- The next step is to repeat the same process with an empty hand. As you cue your dog to Lie Down, I recommend pinching your fingers together (as if you're holding a treat) and doing a similar hand gesture. Once you cue your dog to Lie Down and his shoulder's touch the ground, offer a treat (one you were hiding in your other hand).
- Just as I outlined in the Sit command, once your dog is mastering this command in a quiet room, change up the location.

Look at Me

Teaching your dog to Look is another key command. In certain situations, you'll want to get your dog's attention … and fast. The goal is to master this cue so your dog will look at you no matter what distractions are present.

- Sit on the ground, directly in front of your puppy. The closer you are to your dog, the better.

- Place a treat in front of your eyes, encouraging your dog to look right at you. Once you lock eyes, give the verbal cue, "Look," then offer the tasty reward and praise. Repeat this step several times, gradually holding eye contact for a slightly longer period before giving the treat, so your puppy begins to understand what you want.
- As your dog gets comfortable with this, phase out the treat and work in a hand signal. Get close to your dog and bring your hand up to your eyes, pointing toward your face. As you make eye contact with your dog, give the verbal cue and reward with a treat (one you were hiding in your other hand or pocket) and praise. Repeat this process until your dog gets comfortable.

Stay

Teaching your dog to Stay in one place until he's given a release command is one of the most important things you can do. Not only will you use this cue to raise a well-mannered canine kid who develops patience and self-control, but it's also a life-saver in dangerous situations.

- Standing directly in front of your puppy, show him a treat and direct him into the Sit position. Once sitting, tell him to Stay. Make sure your voice is firm and clear. Pair the verbal cue with a physical cue by holding up one hand with your palm out, as if you're motioning to stop. Wait just a couple seconds and then say a release cue (like "Okay") and offer a treat. Practice this several times, gradually increasing how much time you make your dog wait before offering the treat.

- Once your dog is able to hold a Stay for about 30 seconds, it's time to add distance. Once again, show your dog a treat and direct him into the Sit position. Still holding the treat in front of your dog, give your verbal cue (*"Stay"*) and physical cue (*stop motion*). Then, take one small step back. After just a few seconds, step back in, closer to your dog, give the release cue, and offer a treat and praise. Repeat this step, gradually increasing the number of steps you take each time.

Come

A recall—coming when called—is another potentially life-saving command. Chances are, you'll accidentally drop your puppy's leash or leave the front door open at some point in your dog's life. If your dog comes when called, it will help keep him out of trouble.

- First, pick your reward. If your puppy is food motivated then this may be a high-value treat. If your puppy prefers playtime then your reward may be a squeaky toy.
- Once you have your reward in hand, bring your puppy into a quiet, distraction-free room. Back away from your puppy, leaving a little space in between the two of you. With the treat or toy in one hand, extend it toward your dog and wiggle the reward. In an excited and welcoming tone, invite your puppy to Come. When he comes to you, offer the treat or toy, along with lots of

praise. Repeat this several times, gradually increasing the distance between you and your puppy.

- As your puppy gets comfortable with the Come command, begin practicing in an environment with greater distractions. Whether you're in a room with other people or in your backyard, practice with your puppy on a leash. That way, if he doesn't listen and come when called, you can gently tug on the leash to get his attention.

Drop It

Puppies are curious creatures. As they explore the world for the first time, they will smell, lick, and ultimately try to eat things they shouldn't. If you find your furkid with something poisonous or dangerous in his mouth, knowing this command may save his life.

- A great way to teach your dog the Drop It command is to play tug-of-war. Before you offer your dog his favorite tug toy, make sure you're armed with treats. You'll need these in just a minute!
- Once your dog has a good tug on the toy and you want him to let go, whip out a high-value treat and place it near his nose. As soon as your dog releases the toy, praise him and give the treat. Repeat this step several times, until you feel your dog is responding well.
- Now it's time to add the proper verbal cue. This time during tug, as soon as your dog spots the treat, say "Drop It." Once your pup releases the toy, give the treat. Each time you repeat this step, give the verbal cue earlier.

- Once your dog drops the toy when prompted—before spotting the treat—try the command without the treat. In place of the treat, reward your dog with plenty of praise when he listens.

Leave It

Teaching your dog the Leave It command may help prevent your pup from biting into and ingesting something toxic. Teach this command in steps.

Step 1:

- You'll need two different types of treats: A high-value treat that your dog goes nuts for and a lower-value treat. Make sure to break the treats into tiny pieces so it won't take your puppy long to gobble away.
- Put one type of treat in each hand.
- Place the hand holding the high-value treat behind your back. With your other hand *(the one holding the lower-value treat),* make a fist and extend it toward your puppy. Let him attempt to get the treat. Your puppy will likely sniff, lick, and maybe even paw at your hand.
- When your puppy naturally pulls away, say, "Leave It" and then offer the higher value treat.
- Repeat that process until your puppy immediately stops sniffing your hand when you say, "Leave It."

Step 2:

- Once your dog seems to have a basic understanding of the Leave It command,

repeat the process above with an open hand *(instead of a closed fist).* So, with the lower-value treat resting in your palm, extend your hand toward your puppy. Say, "Leave It." If your puppy actually leaves the treat alone, without attempting to snatch it out of your palm, offer the higher value treat. If your puppy does attempt to snatch the treat from your palm, quickly lift your hand and give a no-reward marker *(i.e. something like "eh-eh").* Give your puppy a few seconds to relax before lowering your hand for another attempt. Repeat that process until your puppy routinely follows the Leave It command.

Step 3:

- Instruct your dog to Sit.
- If you have a small dog, place the lower-value treat on the floor a short distance in front of him. If you have a large dog, place the treat on a chair a short distance in front of him.
- As your hand releases the treat, say, "Leave It." If your dog attempts to take the treat, take it away and give your no-reward marker, such as "eh-eh." Wait a few seconds for your dog to calm down and repeat. Do this until your dog leaves the treat alone. At first, you're looking for your puppy to leave the treat alone for just 5 to 10 seconds. If he does that, offer the high-value reward. Each time you repeat this step, increase the time the treat sits on the floor or chair.

Quick Tips

Stay Consistent – When training a dog, consistency is key. So, make sure everyone in your household is on board with the same house rules. For example, if mom allows dogs on the couch then Fido will be confused if dad gets mad when he's chillin' on the couch.

Also, watch your wording for commands. If you usually tell your dog *Down* when he's jumping on a guest but suddenly tell him to *Get Off* then he isn't going to understand what you want.

Avoid Repeating Commands – Imagine this: You're attempting to teach your pooch the Sit command. So, you grab your treat and instruct him to Sit. But, instead of immediately lowering his booty to the ground, he just stands there looking at you. So, you quickly repeat the word, "Sit." And yet again, "Sit." You may keep saying it five or six times until your pup reacts. Continually repeating a command is just going to stress, frustrate, and even confuse your pup. Plus, we don't want to condition our dogs to only pay attention after we've repeated a word several times. The cue is "Sit"…not "Sit, Sit, Sit."

If Fido ignores your cue, he may not fully understand what you want or he may be too distracted. After calling out a command, remain calm and patient – give him some time to figure it out. If he doesn't listen then take him to a quiet spot and go back to the basics.

Be Mindful About Poisoning Commands – Just like it sounds, this means you accidentally tie a cue to something negative, so your dog eventually stops responding. For example, you've finally mastered the Come command, but you only use it when you're about to give your dog a bath or get in the car to go to the vet. Eventually, your pup may stop coming when called because he knows something not-so-fun is about to happen. When your puppy is first learning commands, keep things positive, and avoid pairing it with something he doesn't like.

Keep Training Sessions Short – Puppies have short attention spans, so cap training sessions to just a few minutes. I usually recommend 10 to 15 minutes max, but, if you have a really young puppy who gasses out at just five minutes then stop there. Be patient with your furkid, as every dog learns at a different pace. If at any point you notice you or your dog getting frustrated, call out one last simple command (*a slam dunk to end on a high note*) and then move on to something else.

6 TIPS TO MASTER LOOSE LEASH WALKING

Training your puppy to walk on a leash is the first step toward being able to take him places. Once your pooch gets comfortable with the leash, you can go on walks around your neighborhood, bring him along to local stores, take him on hikes, etc. Mastering leash training is vital!

Let me start by saying each dog is different. Some take to the leash immediately, while others can't stand it. Some dogs will keep turning around to bite it and others will tug.

Leash training my Diego was somewhat of a nightmare. As a young puppy, he didn't want any part of it. He would tug on it, bite it, spin around and get tangled up in it. He would do anything but walk! On the flip side, my Gigi mastered the leash within just one training session.

Check out the following six tips to help your dog master leash training in no time.

Choose the Right Collar and Leash

Before your dog even takes his first walk on the leash, make sure you have the right equipment.

First, your dog needs a collar or harness. As I mentioned in Chapter 1, I personally prefer a harness to avoid tension on the neck. Plus, during the training phase, I also like to use a front-clip harness. It makes it harder for your dog to pull because, if he does, he'll be forced to turn around.

You'll also need a basic leash (not a retractable leash) that is suitable for your dog's size. You don't want to use a thin leash designed for small breeds if you're walking a large dog (and vice-versa).

Introduce the Leash

Before you hook your puppy's leash onto his collar or harness for the first time, show it to him. Let him sniff and explore. Then, once he stops sniffing, go ahead and clip it on. Give your puppy lots of verbal praise and a treat. It's all about positive reinforcement and making your pup feel secure. You never want your dog to view the leash as scary or bad.

Try Walking With the Leash Inside

Walking outside is rather distracting for your young puppy. After all, there are so many stimulating sights and intriguing smells. To eliminate that distraction, try walking your dog from one room of your house to another (while he's wearing his leash, of course).

Start by standing with your dog in the Heel position (AKA by your side). Next, reward him for being in that position. Then, take your first step. If your puppy steps with you and stays in the Heel position then give him another treat. When you're starting out, go step by step. Reward him after every step once he rests in the Heel position.

Take It Outside

Now that your dog has experienced the leash indoors, it's time to take things outside. But, rather than lacing up your sneakers, clipping on the leash, and heading out for a long walk, my advice is to go slow. Spend a few minutes right outside your home to work on your communication skills. Get your dog to make eye contact with you, priming him to listen to your cues. Use treats!

Is Your Pup Pulling?: If your dog starts tugging and pulling on the leash during your walk, the best thing you can do is simply stop walking. Remain quiet and let your dog keep struggling to pull until he settles down. This may take a few minutes. Once your furbaby settles down, give him a lot of praise and a treat. Eventually, he will associate a loose leash with getting a prize.

Praise, Praise, Praise

I've mentioned the importance of rewarding your furbaby with verbal praise and tasty treats in previous steps. But I really can't stress this enough. A sweet-sounding *good girl* or *good boy* coupled with a drool-worthy snack can go a long way.

Have Patience

Leash training your pup can be frustrating. At times, your dog will pull you in one direction and you'll want to pull him in the opposite direction. Just stay calm and have patience. Don't yank him or yell at him. Dogs can pick up on your emotions. If you're stressed out, they'll become stressed out. Also, remember your dog wants to make you happy. He just needs to understand what you want!

CHAPTER 5

Puppy Biting: This Too (th) Shall Pass

One of the first things that come to mind when I think back to the puppy stage: Those razor-sharp teeth. Puppies love to explore the world with their mouths and play-bite. Plus, they're teething. So, it's pretty common for them to sink their 28 little daggers into practically anything, and I'm not just talking about dog toys and bones. That *anything* also includes your hands, feet, shoes, furniture, wall molding, etc.

If you've just entered the teething phase and your puppy is nipping a lot then you're likely wondering, "How long is this going to last?!" The good news: This too(th) shall pass!

Puppy Teeth Timeline

- Birth: No teeth yet.
- 2–4 weeks: Puppy teeth start coming in.
- 6–7 weeks: Baby teeth should be in by this point. Puppies usually have about 28 baby teeth total.
- 3–4 months: Baby teeth begin to loosen and fall out. While you may find some around your home, puppies often swallow their baby teeth when they're eating or playing.
- 4–6 months: By this point, all baby teeth should have fallen out and most puppies have their full set of adult teeth. In general, adult dogs have about 42 teeth.

If you notice any puppy teeth remaining once young Fido passes six months old, consult with your veterinarian. They may need to be removed.

OUCH! SURVIVING THE TEETHING PHASE

Once your puppy reaches three to four months old, his puppy teeth will begin to fall out, making room for his 42 adult teeth. This process is painful for your pup. As his new teeth start poking through, he'll experience some seriously sore gums. In an effort to soothe the pain, your puppy will chew on anything and everything.

While you certainly don't want to encourage inappropriate chewing and destruction, don't yell or punish your puppy. Don't bite him back (yeah, some people actually recommend that). Instead, communicate with your puppy and redirect his attention.

Communication

When (not if, but when) your puppy nips your hand, many trainers recommend letting out a high-pitched ouch or eh-eh. The theory behind this: It's similar to how your puppy's littermates acted when he bit them a little too hard. Since puppies don't always realize how hard they nip when playing, if they accidentally hurt one of their littermates, the puppy will yelp. So, by letting out a high-pitched ouch or eh-eh, you're communicating in a similar way. Once your puppy releases his grip, praise him for his corrected behavior. This is something I did with all of my puppies and it really helped.

Chew On This

You always have to be one step ahead of your puppy. If you know he's in the biting stage—whether he's teething or play biting—it's important to remain armed with durable toys and appropriate chews. That way, if your puppy is chewing on you, or you catch him gnawing on something he shouldn't, you can redirect his attention to something more appropriate. Here are some of my favorite teething chews:

KONG Puppy Teething Stick—KONG is a popular brand that's known for its durable dog toys. They have an entire line of rubber toys designed specifically for puppies! Their puppy teething stick is meant to soothe a teething puppy's gums. Along with giving your pup something to gnaw on, this thick rubber stick features strategically placed grooves that help clean teeth.

Classic KONG—The Classic KONG is made with the same durable rubber as their teething stick, but this design features a stuffable hole in the center. Fill that center with some high-value treats or food and give it to your pup. Bump it up a notch by stuffing and then freezing the KONG, since the cold will help soothe your puppy's gums. I share my 3-step DIY KONG stuffing recipe on page 135.

Chilly Bone—Speaking of frozen teething toys, this special dog toy that's shaped like a bone is designed to be soaked in water and then popped in the freezer for several hours, or overnight.

Rope Toys—If you can't find the Chilly Bone then you can do something similar with a rope toy. Rope toys are pretty hard to destroy, easy to clean, and affordable. They're also easy to soak in water and freeze for your pup. Warning: Rope toys are made *of multiple strands of thin fabric all woven together. If your dog is an intense player and wears these strands down then Fido can ingest them, causing damage and/or a blockage in the digestive tract. So, monitor your dog closely when playing with rope toys and pick them up when playtime is over.*

Hard Frozen Veggies—Carrots make for a super healthy dog treat and, if you freeze them, they can also help soothe your puppy's gums as he gnaws.

Bully Stick—Now we're bringing out the big guns! Dogs of all ages love bully sticks and they're a better option than many other chews since they're softer and digestible. *Stay clear of antlers (which are way too hard for puppy teeth and can easily leave a chipped tooth) and rawhides (which come with a long list of health risks).* Another benefit of bully sticks: They're just one ingredient. These popular chew sticks are made from bull penis. I know, I know—it's pretty gross when you think about it. But, what can I say, dogs love um'!

Bully sticks come in several forms: Straight, braided, curled, and rings. Whichever you choose, just make sure to supervise your

puppy and pick it up when playtime is over. When dogs whittle down a stick to just one or two inches, it becomes a choking hazard. To avoid potential risk, look into a bully stick holder. It's a genius product that firmly holds onto the chew stick, preventing a pup from swallowing any bits once it's whittled down to an unsafe size.

Bye-Bye Toy Boredom

If your puppy seems bored with the same old toys, it's probably because he is! Imagine this: There's a big pile of dog toys on one end of the room. It's the same pile of toys that's always there. Then, you come walking in and slip off your shoes. *Something new!* Which do you think is more appealing to your puppy? Yup—those new, shiny shoes.

Instead of keeping your puppy's teething toys accessible all day, reserve them for special moments *(i.e. moments you want your dog's teeth to get the heck off your hand, furniture, and wall moldings!)*.

When you bust out the special teething toys, wiggle them around to entice your pup. You can even play tug-of-war, just keep it gentle since your puppy's teeth are still maturing.

An Impromptu Training Session

Here's another redirection idea. Next time your puppy nibbles on your hand when he's trying to interact with you, grab some high-value treats, and start an impromptu training session. This is the perfect time to work on those commands from the last chapter. But, wait. Are you worried your dog will associate the treat with his earlier biting? Don't be! Puppies live in the moment. Once you instruct your puppy to Sit, Lie Down, Come, or Stay, your puppy will connect the positive reward to that command.

More Teething Tips

- If you can't keep an eye on baby Fido, confine him in a crate or exercise pen. Refer to the crate training guide on page 29.
- Along with proper training and a plethora of appropriate toys, spraying something bitter onto your furniture may help deter your dog from inappropriate chewing. While you can buy Bitter Apple spray from a retailer, you can easily make a cheaper and healthier version at home. Try spraying a simple 2:1 mixture of apple cider vinegar and white vinegar.

7 Signs Your Dog's Teeth Need More Attention

- Visible plaque and tartar build-up
- Stinky breath
- Bleeding gums
- Loose teeth

- Changes in eating habits
- Constantly licking the air
- Pawing at the mouth

WHY CARING FOR YOUR DOG'S ADULT TEETH IS IMPORTANT

Once your puppy's adult teeth have made their grand debut, it's your job to keep them pearly white and healthy. Unfortunately, more than 80% of dogs over the age of three reportedly suffer from active dental disease. Unless pet parents take action early on, their dog's teeth will just worsen with age, eventually impacting overall health.

It all starts with the mouth. Within just a few hours of eating a meal, plaque can start forming on the teeth. Within just 24 hours, that gummy plaque can accumulate, mineralize, and harden, becoming tartar. Forming above and below the gum line, tartar irritates the gums and can lead to inflammation (*AKA gingivitis*). Swollen, red, and even bleeding gums are not normal and need to be checked by a veterinarian.

This all causes some pretty stinky dog breath and can leave your pooch in a lot of pain. Eventually, if poor dental health progresses, the teeth can rot, loosen, and likely fall out. But it doesn't end there.

Dogs who suffer from poor dental health typically have weakened and broken down gum tissue. This creates *openings* in the gums for bacteria to enter the bloodstream. If your dog's immune system doesn't fight off that bacteria, it can reach and eventually affect the heart. Periodontal disease can also trigger serious health issues in other organs, such as the liver and kidneys.

YOUR GUIDE TO DOGGY TOOTHBRUSHING

Daily toothbrushing is one of the best ways you can keep your dog's teeth pearly white. I promise it's not a time-consuming task. But spending a few minutes each day to clean your dog's chompers will provide him many benefits throughout his lifetime.

Step 1: Get Your Dog Used to His Lips Being Touched

Before you jump right into brushing your dog's teeth, spend a few days gently massaging his lips. Simply rub your fingers in a small circular motion across his gum line and teeth. You don't need to do this for a long time—just once or twice a day for about 10 to 15 seconds.

Step 2: Introduce the Toothpaste

Toothpaste's texture is unlike anything your dog has ever eaten before. So he needs a little time to get used to it. Start by placing a very small amount of pet-formulated toothpaste (*never use your own toothpaste on a dog*) onto your finger and let your dog lick it off. If he doesn't seem interested then gently dab a very small amount of it on his lips. Do this for a few days in a row.

Not only will this step help your pooch get used to the texture of toothpaste, but also the taste. There are several pet-toothpaste flavors to choose from, such as poultry, beef, or vanilla mint. If your dog doesn't seem to like one, try another.

Step 3: Introduce a Gauze Pad and Brushes

Now that your pooch is familiar with toothpaste, it's time to introduce the brush. I recommend starting with a small gauze pad since it's a little less intimidating than a full-on toothbrush.

Show your dog the gauze pad—let him smell and investigate it for a moment. Then, lift his lip to expose the outside surfaces of his gums and teeth, and wipe them with the gauze.

Once your pooch seems comfortable with the gauze pad, move on to a finger brush or soft bristle toothbrush made for dogs. Repeat the same process—first allowing him to smell the brush and then pretending to actually brush the teeth.

Step 4: Get Brushing for Real

It's finally time to brush your puppy's teeth!

Using your cleaning tool of choice (*gauze pad, finger brush, or toothbrush*), apply a small dab of pet-formulated toothpaste. Lift your puppy's lip to expose the outside surfaces of his gums and teeth and begin brushing. Make gentle, small, circular motions, similar to how you would brush your own teeth.

Along with cleaning the front teeth, make sure to reach back by the molars, since those are usually the dirtiest. When you're brushing, focus on the outside of your pet's teeth—that's where most of the tartar and plaque builds up. The average canine won't allow us to brush the inner surface of their teeth, but once you're done and your dog licks his lips, he'll naturally move some of that toothpaste to that area.

Tip: Don't Rush and Stay Calm

When you first start brushing your dog's teeth, don't rush the process. If your dog is only comfortable with getting a few teeth brushed at a time then only brush a few at a time. You can break up cleaning sessions—brushing in the morning and at night.

Tip: Reward

Since your puppy's teeth are freshly cleaned, I would refrain from rewarding him with food. But, once you finish brushing, definitely offer a lot of verbal praise and petting!

No, Kibble Doesn't Clean Your Dog's Teeth!

At some point, you'll undoubtedly hear someone say: "*You don't have to brush your dog's teeth if he eats hard kibble.*" The thought behind this is that crunching down on kibble will naturally scrape the teeth clean. I only have one thing to say about that: Not true! Regular dry kibble doesn't clean your dog's teeth any more than cereal, pretzels, or potato chips clean yours. When you eat cereal (*or your dog eats kibble*) tiny food particles are left behind and stick to the teeth. If they aren't brushed away, plaque forms, and that vicious cycle I mentioned a minute ago begins.

CHAPTER 6:

Lookin' Spiffy

Just like we carve out time each day to wash our bodies, comb our hair, and brush our teeth, our canine companions need some regular primping too. Sure, some dog breeds require more grooming than others. My short-hair Chihuahua is a breeze compared to my toy poodle. But, all dogs require some pampering from time to time.

PUPPY PEDICURE

Tap, tap, tap. Are those your puppy's nails tapping on the floor? If so, it's time to trim those babies! Unlike our trips to the salon for a fresh coat of polish, puppy pedicures aren't cosmetic. When a dog's nails tap on hard surfaces, it pushes their nails up into their nail beds, which can be painful. Not only does it put pressure on the toe joints, but it can also force the toes to twist to the side, resulting in soreness or even arthritis.

Before you grab the clippers and start trimming, let's chat about basic nail anatomy. *I know that doesn't sound too fun, but it's important.*

The hard, outer part of your puppy's nails is called the *shell*, and inside is a pink nerve called the *quick*. The quick supplies blood to the nail and, during trims, your goal is to leave the quick fully intact. If you cut this part, you'll immediately hear your dog shriek in pain and you'll see blood.

If your dog has white nails then it's pretty easy to spot the quick *(as you can see in the photo on the next page)*. Over time, you'll notice regular nail trims cause the quicks to recede *(short quicks are ideal)*. If your dog has black nails, though, you won't see the quick through the shell. This certainly makes trims a bit more complicated, but not impossible.

Tools

If your dog regularly walks and plays on rough surfaces—like concrete—you *may* not have to cut his nails often, since the hard surface will wear them down naturally. With that said, most dogs need a nail trim every two to four weeks. To trim your dog's nails you'll need:

High-Quality Set of Dog Nail Clippers or a Grinder—A high-quality set of dog nail clippers can make a huge difference. Cheap clippers can leave your dog's nails cracked and crooked. When looking for a quality clipper, you'll notice two different styles:

scissor-style *(which works like a pair of scissors)* and guillotine-style *(where a blade lowers and slices off the nail)*. I personally prefer the scissor-style clippers.

If you and/or your dog is extremely afraid of the clippers, you may prefer using a grinder, which is a tool that files your dog's nail. For my Chihuahua, I use regular scissor-style clippers, but my poodle is way more cooperative with the grinder. She just seems to prefer the feeling.

Styptic Powder—If you accidentally cut too far, this will help clot the quick and stop the bleeding.

Nail File—If you use a traditional clipper versus a grinder, you may feel some sharp edges left over on your dog's nails. Use a nail file to smooth them.

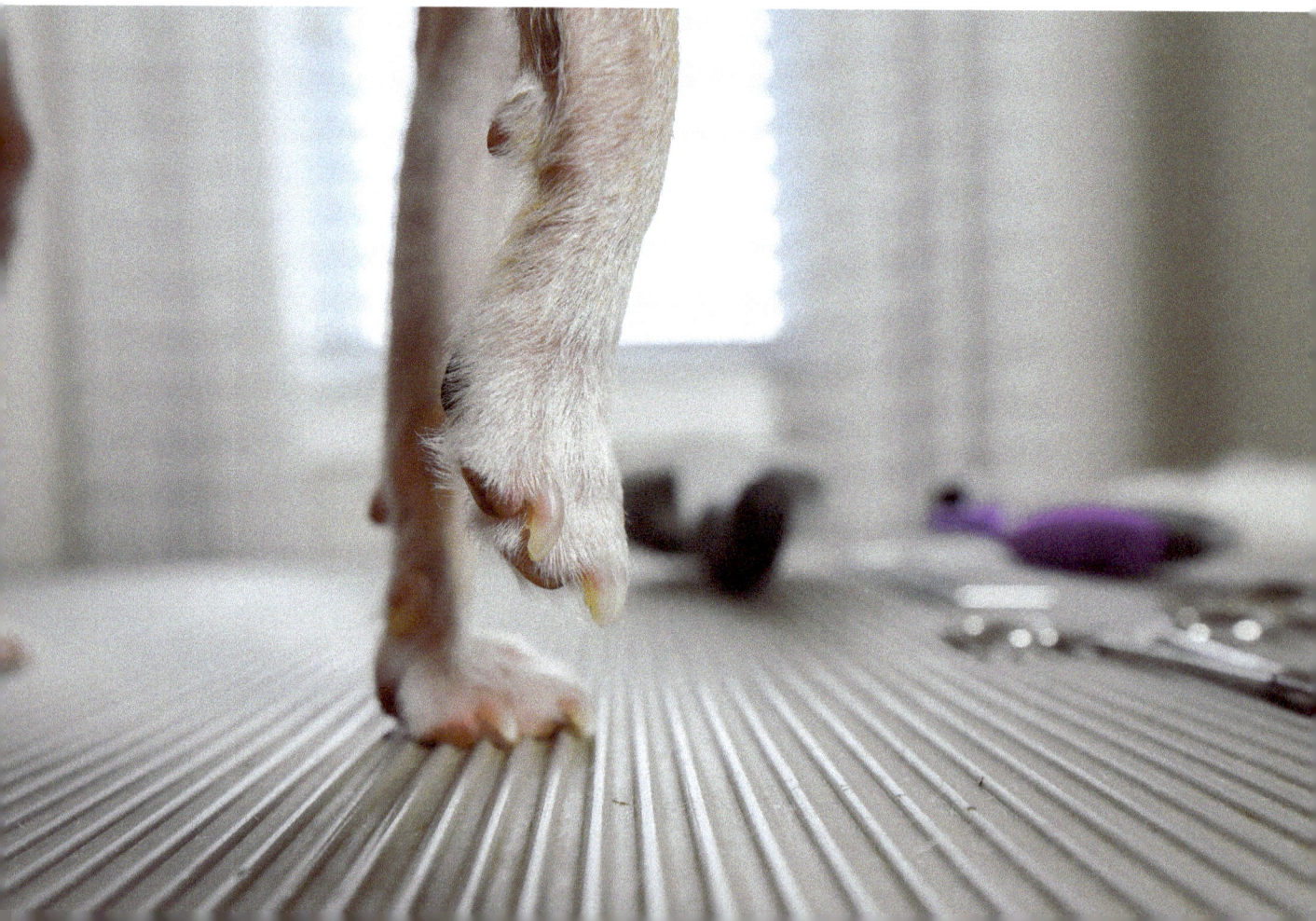

Getting Your Dog Comfortable

I know *hate* is a strong word, but a lot of dogs *hate* having their paws touched. So, while you have a young puppy on your hands, this is the perfect time to desensitize. Here are some tips to get your dog more comfortable with you handling his paws, and ultimately clipping his nails:

- From the first day you bring your puppy home, frequently touch and hold his paws. If your pup seems relaxed, give him a treat.
- Before clipping your puppy's nails, show him the clipper or grinder. Let him sniff and explore, and give him a treat and praise for doing so.
- Next, gently touch the clipper or grinder *(turned off)* to each paw. Give a treat and praise. Repeat this step several times.
- Once your dog seems comfortable with the last step, place the clippers around his nail, but don't actually clip. Remove and give a treat and praise. If you're using a grinder instead of clippers, turn it on briefly so your pup can hear its sound. Only keep it on for a few seconds and don't actually touch it to your dog's nails. Give a treat and praise.
- Try trimming one nail, clipping off just a small piece to get your dog used to the feeling. Give a treat and praise. Don't rush this process and work your way up to a full nail trim.

Clipping White Dog Nails

1. Hold your dog's paw firmly, but gently.
2. Place clippers around the tip of your dog's nail—below the quick at a 45° angle.

3. Double-check the clippers aren't on top of the quick. If you're in the clear, snip off the tip of the nail.
4. If your dog's nail starts bleeding that means you hit the quick. If this happens, immediately press your dog's nail into a bottle of styptic powder to clot the cut.
5. Don't forget to cut the dewclaws. *(Along with the toenails found in the front of your pup's paws, dogs are also born with a toenail on the inside of their front legs. They're called dewclaws and they're essentially doggy thumbs. In some breeds, the dewclaws are removed, but, the majority of dogs will have them. So, take a quick peek and if your pup has them, make sure to trim those too.)*
6. Lightly file your puppy's nails to eliminate any sharp edges.
7. Reward your pooch with treats and affection.

Cutting Black Nails

While cutting white nails is typically done with one cut per nail, that's not the case for black nails. The trick is to make several very shallow cuts, pausing between each one to check the cut surface. If the cut surface appears whitish, it's safe to trim a little bit more. When you're about to approach the quick, the nail's cut surface will appear black. So, once you see black, stop!

Grinding Nails

1. Hold your dog's nail firmly, but gently.
2. Turn the grinder on and place it on the bottom of your dog's nail *(by the tip)*. Lightly apply pressure for no more than three to five seconds at a time. Remain mindful of any sensitivity and frequently remove the grinder to check your progress.

HAIR FOR DAYS

Tangles, knots, and mats…oh my! If you're raising a medium or long-haired pooch then chances are you've dealt with knots before. Even the most diligent pet parent who regularly combs their pup's coat will find themselves head to head with a stubborn mat at some point. When you spot a knot, though, it's important to bust out your grooming tools and work through it ASAP. If ignored, little tangles can grow into large, nasty mats. Not only is it frustrating for you, but it's also extremely uncomfortable for your pooch.

Most Common Areas Tangles and Mats Form

- Ears
- Under the arms
- Along the back of the legs
- Under the belly
- Below the neck

This may differ depending on your dog's breed. For example, if I don't run a comb through the top of Gigi's head every single day, her hair tangles. But, since she has a shaved belly, she never gets knots there. It all depends on your dog.

Have the Right Grooming Tools Handy

There are several different grooming tools on the market that can help break up your dog's tangles, knots, and mats. I personally keep a little arsenal of brushes and combs that include the following:

- Slicker brush — Start with a slicker brush to help identify various tangles and mats in your dog's coat.
- Steel comb — Use a steel comb to continue locating mats and begin to gently work them out.
- Mat remover — Bust out a de-matting rake to break up super stubborn mats.

Along with preventing tangles, knots, and mats, regular hair brushing also helps to spread natural oils throughout the coat and allow for a flea/tick check.

While short-haired dogs require much less maintenance, if your pooch sheds, you'll benefit from a de-shedding brush. I run one through Diego's hair several times a week and notice a huge difference in his coat. It feels better and I find way fewer loose hairs lying around my home. *Win-win!*

SPLISH SPLASH, THERE'S A DOG IN THE BATH

Scrubb-a-dub-dub…is it time to pop your pooch in the tub? Bath time may not be fun for your dog, but it's extremely important to keep your pooch clean! Some quick tips:

1. Start by brushing your dog's coat thoroughly to remove any mats, as they can worsen once wet.

2. Place a rubber mat at the bottom of the tub to help prevent your dog from slipping.
3. Turn on the water, adjust the temperature to a comfortable lukewarm, put your pooch in the tub, and wet your dog. Keep the drain open, as you don't want to fill the tub with water.

4. Using a pet-formulated shampoo, start at your dog's neck and work your way down his body. Get a nice lather around your dog's neck, back, booty, legs, and paws.

5. Before you turn off the bathwater, make sure all of the soap is rinsed out of your dog's coat.

6. Time to dry! Start with a quick towel-dry *(opt for a super absorbent microfiber towel over a traditional towel)* and then move on to a blowdry with a professional dog dryer.

7. Once your pooch is dry, brush his coat again to ensure there aren't any leftover tangles.

8. Reward with treats and praise!

Common Mistakes Pet Parents Make During Bath Time

Before you grab your towel, run the bathwater, and give your four-legged love a good cleaning, check out this list of common bath time mistakes.

Not Checking the Temperature — Do you like getting sprayed with freezing cold or scalding hot water? Well, neither does your dog! Before you pop your pup in the tub for a bath, make sure to adjust the water until you reach a nice lukewarm temperature. Test out the temperature by spraying water on the inside of your forearm first, since that area is more sensitive to hot/cold than your hands.

Not Protecting Your Dog's Eyes and Ears — Even dogs who seem to enjoy their time in the tub don't want water sprayed in their eyes and ears.

The Eyes

If water gets in your dog's eyes, it can be extremely uncomfortable and even a bit painful. To avoid a potential accident, when it comes time to wash your pup's face, I recommend sticking to a wet washcloth. That way you have full control over where the water and shampoo wind up.

The Ears

Water in your dog's ears can lead to infection. To keep your dog's ears clean, use either a damp washcloth or ear wipes made specifically for dogs, and wipe the ears clean. Don't go too far into the ear and never stick Q-tips down the ear canal.

Using a Super Strong Spray — Many of us rely on a handheld showerhead or bath faucet to wash our canine companions. The only problem? If you have super strong water pressure then it may frighten your pooch and/or cause some discomfort. For my two small dogs, I usually spray the bathtub faucet water into a plastic cup and then dump the cup of water onto my dogs' bodies. But, an easier solution for large dogs is to let the water hit the back of your hand first, reducing the pressure before it hits your dog's skin.

Not Using the Right Shampoo — As tempting as it is to share your human shampoo with your pooch, it's best to stick with a formula specifically for canines. Talk to a local groomer to help you find the perfect shampoo for your pup.

Washing Your Dog Too Much *(Or Not Enough)* — This really depends on what products you use. If you use a harsh shampoo weekly then you can actually strip away the natural oils in your pet's coat and cause skin irritation. However, there are products on the market that make regular baths easier on your pooch. Speak with your groomer or veterinarian to determine the best products and schedule for your dog's breed!

Not Drying Your Pooch Well—When bath time is over, it's important to take the time to dry off your dog. With an absorbent towel, gently squeeze his fur (*not skin*) to pull out as much water as possible. For short-haired dogs, the towel will likely be enough. But if you have a medium or long-haired dog, you may want to invest in a professional grooming dryer to finish up the drying process.

Yelling or Scolding—Bath time can be stressful for your pooch. And, while I understand dealing with a fussy pup is frustrating, yelling only makes matters worse. Instead, work on positive reinforcement with praise and yummy treats. *Oh, the power of food!*

GETTING YOUR DOG COMFORTABLE WITH THE BLOW DRYER

I've been home grooming my Gigi for several years. If you ask me, investing in a professional blow dryer that's made specifically for dogs makes a huge difference. Some pros: The temperature-control means it doesn't run as hot as many human hairdryers, which is important to avoid burns. The powerful airflow dries hair quickly and thoroughly. Plus, it gives dog hair a much nicer finish! To put it simply, there's really no comparison to your personal hairdryer.

But, while we may be impressed by these amazing drying machines, our dogs feel otherwise. The loud noise and extreme blasts of air can be super scary to Fido—especially if he's not used to it. So, before you fire up the doggy blow dryer and blast away the water droplets, it's important to take the time to desensitize your pup.

Step 1: Sniff It ... Sniff It Real Good
Before you even turn on the blow dryer, give your dog time to explore. In a closed room, with both your pup and the dryer on the ground, let him sniff away. As he gets closer and shows some interest, offer up high-value treats and praise. This will help your dog associate the dryer with something positive.

Step 2: Go Low
Next, the goal is to get your dog familiar with, and desensitized to, the loud noise. So, with the dryer nozzle pointed away from your dog (*preferably near the ground*) and your dog up on the grooming table, turn the dryer onto its lowest setting. Before your dog even has a chance to react, immediately turn the dryer off and give him a treat.

Repeat, leaving the dryer on for about 10 seconds. Repeat again, leaving the dryer on for about 30 seconds. As you allow the dryer to run for longer increments, offer high-value treats while it's turned on.

Step 3: A Closer Look
Once your dog is comfortable with the sound from afar, it's time to move the dryer hose closer. Keeping the dryer on its lowest setting, hold the nozzle with one hand. Point the dryer nozzle down toward the ground and away from Fido. In your other hand, hold several small treats. Slowly move your treat-filled hand closer to your dog and start offering him snacks, one by one. As your dog munches away, if he seems comfortable, bring the dryer a bit closer and closer.

If your dog is too nervous to accept treats, rely on soft petting and verbal praise instead. Don't scold or force your frightened dog, as that will just add to his stress. Instead, stay calm and go slow. Depending on how comfortable your dog gets, you may need to repeat this step for a few days before moving on to an actual groom.

Step 4: A Slight Breeze

Now it's time to run the blower over your dog *(starting near his back/sides)* and let him feel the air. Just like in Step 2, start with a few seconds and gradually work your way up.

Step 5: Aim High

Once your dog is comfortable with the blow dryer on a low setting, repeat Steps 3 and 4 with high settings. Since these blowers are really strong, make sure you have a good grip on the hose/nozzle. If you don't, you may lose hold of it and it will whip around and scare your pup. *I say this from experience.*

HAPPINESS IS A FRESH HAIRCUT

Since every dog breed has different trimming needs, and this isn't a grooming book, I'm not going very in-depth here. If you're interested in home-grooming your pup, I definitely recommend watching some videos online made by professional groomers *(there are some amazing free tutorials for each breed)* and consulting with a local groomer. But, since I do get asked about this subject all the time, I've included a quick cheat-sheet filled with tips worth knowing.

- If you're planning to invest in buzzer clippers, splurge on a high-quality pair. You can absolutely tell the difference between a $50 and $300 pair of clippers. Sure, the initial bill isn't fun to pay. But, they last a really long time! The clippers I use have been in my family for more than a decade, and still going strong. Look into brands like Wahl *(I love their cordless Arco clippers)* and Andis.
- When it comes to clipper blades, remember this: The higher the number, the closer the shave/the shorter the cut. *I personally use* a 5 on Gigi's body and a 10 on her face *(because my goal is a closer shave).*
- Unlike with human haircuts, which usually happen on wet hair, dogs get trims after a blowdry.
- When buzzing your dog's body, clip in the direction the hair is growing. For example, when clipping the top of your dog's back *(along the spine)*, you'll work from their neck to the base of the tail. But, as you shave down and around your dog's body *(closer to their sides)*, be mindful that hair growth can change directions. You would buzz down the legs, not up. Down the front of the neck and belly, not up. So, always pay attention to the way the hair is growing to ensure a smooth cut.
- If you have a dog breed that requires a buzzed face, gently hold their snout closed when working close to the mouth to avoid accidental tongue cuts. My mom and I learned that the hard way. Growing up, she

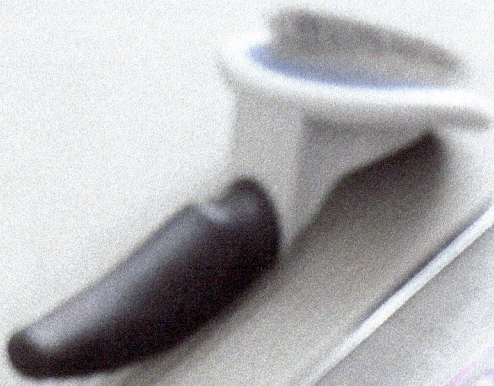

used to groom our poodles in between professional appointments, and, one day, she accidentally clipped a tongue. Blood everywhere!

- Clippers can overheat. So, throughout your home haircut, continually check the blade temperature to avoid skin burns. Once the blade is hot, either use a clipper cooling spray, swap out the blade for a fresh one, or take a break.

- Along with clippers, you'll likely use scissors during home haircuts. There are various types on the market and they all have their purpose. For me, I use a curved scissor to shape my poodle's round top knot and straight scissors to help clean up her legs. There are also blending and thinning scissors *(which look like a cross between a pair of scissors and a hair comb)* to help smooth and thin out a dog's heavy coat.

My best advice? Spend time educating yourself, get the right tools, and have patience. Every time I groom Gigi, I get better and better. It's about taking your time and staying calm.

Warning Signs It's Time to Change Groomers

I'm Gigi's personal groomer, tending to her every misplaced hair and overgrown nail. But, that wasn't always the case. I decided to take on that task after a scarring experience left her anxiety-ridden.

I remember it like it was yesterday. Pulling up to the grooming shop and my Gigi shaking in fear. As I reached for the car door handle, she wiggled and squirmed out of my arms. It was her attempt to run away from what was about to happen.

We left the car and I carried her into the grooming shop. With my arms wrapped around her little body, I felt her heart beating right out of her chest. The groomer greeted me with a smile and I handed her my messy pooch. A few hours later, it was back to the grooming shop to pick up a freshly trimmed and gorgeous Gigi. Her tail wagged a mile a minute and the excitement to leave was written all over her face.

This exact scenario played out once a month for about six months. I'm ashamed it took me that long to realize Gigi's actions weren't just a result of separation anxiety. I finally left my former groomer when Gigi came home with burns and cuts all over her face and paws. The groomer had also cut the skin around her anus, making simple things, like walking and going #2, a real challenge for my little girl. Seeing Gigi like that made my heart sink. I finally realized she was being mistreated and I never took her to that shop again.

Here are some warning signs it's time to change groomers:

Extreme Fear

It's normal for dogs to get a little nervous when they first arrive at their grooming shop. After all, dogs don't look forward to baths, loud hairdryers, and buzzing clippers. But extreme fear, like my Gigi's, should serve as a red flag. So, when you arrive at your grooming shop, watch your dog closely. Does he cry or attempt to run away? Does his heart begin pounding? Is there a general look of fear on his face? Don't ignore these signs!

Burns and Cuts

It's understandable if your dog's skin gets nicked every once in a while. Maybe he wiggled his body at a bad moment. Accidents happen. But if skin burns and cuts are a regular occurrence then it's time to look for grooming services elsewhere. Beauty shouldn't mean pain for our furkids. Ever!

Not Listening to Your Instructions

Have you ever asked your groomer to do one thing and they did the complete opposite? Is this a habit? If so, it's time to go! You should have open communication with your groomer and trust that he/she is going to listen to your instructions.

A General Bad Vibe

When you drop your dog off at the grooming shop, you should feel 100% comfortable and know your furbaby is in good hands. If you find yourself second-guessing your dog's safety or just get the feeling things aren't right then it's time to find another groomer.

Tips to Choose a Reputable & Trusted Groomer

Ask Around

Start with your neighbors, friends, and local family members. Ask who they use and if they're happy with the services. Chances are, if their dogs are treated well and come home looking spiffy then yours will too.

Your veterinarian is also a great resource. Since many reputable grooming facilities require vaccination records from your vet, your doggy doctor should have a list of trusted groomers. Your vet may even offer grooming services right there in the office.

You can also take your search online. Post a question on NextDoor, your community's Facebook page, or check review sites.

Check for Certifications

While I've been to some amazing groomers who aren't certified, this is one thing you may want to check. Many reputable groomers hold a grooming certification, which means they've passed both written and practical exams by an accredited grooming school.

Take a Tour of the Shop

Before your puppy's first grooming appointment at a new shop, schedule a tour so you can meet the groomer and scope out the environment. A few things to look for:

- Does the place look clean?
- Do the dogs look happy?
- Does the staff seem knowledgeable and caring?
- Is the staff handling their canine customers gently?
- Are dogs waiting in crates or has the groomer set up space for them to run free?
- Does the shop use kennel dryers? If so, are they set on a timer, and is someone constantly monitoring the dogs to ensure they aren't overheating?
- Do the groomers work in a closed-off/private room or are their grooming tables set up in a visible space? Ideally, the groomers will work in an open area or space that's

lined with windows, allowing puppy parents to watch the entire grooming process. Transparency is key!

Another tip: Bring your dog along for the tour to help get him acclimated.

Ask Questions

Don't hesitate to ask your potential groomer questions! Some to consider:

- How long has the grooming facility been in operation?
- Does the groomer attend grooming trade shows and seminars to keep up with the newest products, trends, and handling procedures?
- Is the groomer certified?
- Does the grooming shop have a license to operate in the state?
- Is the groomer familiar with your dog's breed and specific needs?
- Does the groomer require proof of vaccinations from your vet?
- Does the groomer keep past grooming and medical records?
- What products does the groomer use?
- Does the groomer have a plan in case of a medical emergency?
- How much does the groomer charge?

CHAPTER 7

Yappy Hour

SOCIALIZING YOUR PUPPY

What your dog learns as a young puppy will stick with him for the rest of his life. The prime socialization period is typically 6 to 14 weeks old. During this time, it's important to expose your puppy to as many sights, sounds, and experiences as possible. Unfortunately, this is also a time veterinarians tell us not to take our young puppies out in public because they haven't finished their puppy shots. So, until your pup is protected, you have to get creative.

Let Your Dog Explore Your Home and Backyard

When you first bring your furbaby home, let him explore. *And don't rush this process.* Let his paws walk on—and feel the difference between—carpet, tile, and hardwood floors.

If you have a backyard, where unfamiliar dogs can't access, let your unvaccinated pup experience the grass, dirt, and pavement. Let him sniff around. Watch him closely as he explores all of the new smells, sights, and sounds.

You may be thinking to yourself, *"How the heck does this help socialize my dog with people and other dogs?"* But, look at this as Step 1. Letting your puppy acclimate to different environments will help teach him to easily adapt to new situations.

Gain Your Dog's Trust

When you first bring a new puppy home, make sure to spend a lot of time with him. Work on commands, go for walks, play together, and snuggle up for some naps. This will enhance your bond and teach your pooch to trust.

Sit on Your Front Porch

Whether you live in a neighborhood or apartment complex, if you have a front porch or veranda then consider it a great socialization tool for your young puppy. From a distance, let your puppy watch the world go by. Let him see your neighbors walking the sidewalks or working on their cars. He may see kids whizzing by on bicycles. Plus, along with the sights, your puppy may hear cars starting, bells ringing, music playing, etc. When your pup sees or hears something new and has a positive reaction then give him a treat and verbal praise.

Get Family and Friends Involved

If your puppy can't go to the party then bring the party to your puppy. While you don't want to overwhelm your little one, you still want to expose him to people of different genders, ages, and races while he's still in that prime socialization period. Have one or two family members over for the afternoon to play with your new canine kid. When your dog is friendly and engages with new people, make sure to offer lots of praise. You know the drill: Make it a real positive experience.

Schedule Doggy Play Dates

Along with getting your new puppy used to adults, teens, and children, ask a friend to bring their dog over for a little playdate. Make sure you trust the other dog and he's a similar size.

Go for Walks Around Your Community

When your vet says it's safe to take your puppy out in public, start by walking him around your community or apartment complex. Get him even more familiar with the faces and environment he'll be exposed to regularly. Stop to greet friendly neighbors, enjoy some puppy petting, and don't forget to bring the treats along to reward good behavior.

Go for Car Rides (and Take Him into Dog-Friendly Shops)

Again, the point is to get your dog used to seeing different people, animals, and scenarios. Expose your dog to people who are wearing hats and sunglasses. Let him see tall people and short people; heavy people and skinny people. If you're taking a quick trip to the store, either bring a friend or family member along so your dog can sit in the parking lot and people watch *or* take him inside dog-friendly shops.

> NOTE: Don't leave your dog in the car alone while you run errands and go shopping. Cars can quickly overheat or become too cold. If a friend can't come with you or your dog can't come inside then it's best to leave him home.

Puppy Training Classes

Training classes are two-fold—they're great for socializing with other dogs and you get to work on basic training.

Organize a Dog Walking Group

Either through your community's Facebook page or Meetup app, organize a little group of dedicated dog parents and their friendly pups. Weekly or monthly pack walks are a great way for both you and your furkid to make new friends.

DOG PARK SAFETY TIPS

I'm not a huge fan of dog parks, especially for young puppies. Sure, on one hand, the dog park offers our furkids a place to run off-leash, burn off excess energy, and socialize with new furry friends. But, as someone who used to take her dogs to the dog park, I can tell you from experience , they're also a place where many puppies pick up bad habits. It's not uncommon to see dog fights breakout. That's not to mention, it's also a breeding ground for disease. Not only are a bunch of random dogs going to the bathroom in the same enclosed area *(and you'll always spot at least one person who doesn't pick up after their pooch)*, you have no clue if those other dogs are up-to-date on their vaccines. While I advise against off-leash dog parks, if you do plan to visit one at some point in your pup's life, it's important to keep these safety tips in mind:

Vaccinations

It's important to protect your pup before stepping foot *(or paw)* inside those park gates. We'll go over vaccinations thoroughly in the next chapter!

Training

Anything can happen at a dog park, so it's essential to master a few basic commands—like Look, Come, Stay, and Drop It—before your visit. If you're set on taking your canine kid to the dog park, but concerned he won't have good park etiquette, keep him on a leash. Look into getting a longline leash so you can give your pup more slack at times. This is a great way to maintain control while still letting your dog feel a little freedom.

Pack for the Occasion

- Your dog's leash *(and a backup leash)*
- Poop bags *(in case the dispensers are empty)*
- Water bottle
- Water bowl *(I was never a fan of my dogs sharing a water bowl with unfamiliar dogs. So, while most parks have a bowl of water sitting out for the canine visitors, I preferred to pack my own.)*
- Frisby, ball, or another toy
- High-value treats
- Whistle *(this is optional, but it could come in handy to quickly get your dog's attention or distract a dog during tense times)*

Pick the Right Park

Before you take your precious pooch into an off-leash fenced park, take a few minutes to inspect the area. Here are some things to look for:

- Double-gated fence entry for security to cut down on potential escapes.
- Separate area for large dogs and small dogs. Plus, make sure people are actually obeying the large dog/small dog sides. In the park I used to visit, I would occasionally see people bring their very large dog into the small dog section. When this happened, I would leave because I didn't feel 100% comfortable.
- Well-stocked poop bag dispensers and garbage cans scattered throughout the

park. Also, make sure puppy parents are actually using them and picking up after their canine kid leaves a present. Dog poop is known to host a multitude of parasites, bacteria, and viruses. Some of those poop piles could contain hookworms, tapeworms, roundworms, whipworms, coccidia, giardia, E. coli, and parvovirus *(just to name a few)*.

Check Out the Other Dogs

Every time you arrive at the dog park, take a few minutes to check out the other dogs. If you notice a dog acting aggressively inside the fenced area, turn around and go home. A little playtime isn't worth the risk. Diego got attacked once and it wasn't a pleasant experience *(obviously)*!

Always Watch Your Pooch

When you're at the dog park, it's easy to get caught up talking to fellow dog parents. *One good thing about the park: It's a great place to meet people!* But don't let this distraction keep you from watching over your dog.

- Someone may have forgotten to close the fence gate
- Your dog may have gone to the bathroom and you need to clean it up
- Your dog may need a drink of water
- Maybe your dog stepped in something he shouldn't have
- Your dog may not be having any fun and wants to leave
- An aggressive dog can always enter the park and a fight can break out in a split second. If you notice another dog growling at your dog *(or your dog is growling at another dog)*, try to stay calm. Clap your hands to get your puppy's attention and call out your recall command.

CHAPTER 8

A Trip to the Vet

Finding the right veterinarian for your new puppy is just as important as finding the right doctor for yourself. Throughout your dog's life, you'll turn to your vet a lot. Along with routine visits, he/she will become your go-to resource whenever you notice something *off* with your pup (*whether he isn't eating or drinking, you've noticed a change in bathroom habits, or maybe he's biting his paws and scratching a lot*).

Since your vet will play a large role in your puppy's life, it's important to do your research and find someone you trust. Start by asking neighbors, friends, and family members who they recommend. Also, spend some time reading online reviews. Check out The American Animal Hospital Association (*accredited clinics means the office is operating at a high level of care*) and Fear Free Pets, another database that helps you find certified hospitals with a common goal of alleviating the stress and anxiety associated with a vet visit. Once a particular office seems like a good fit, don't hesitate to call and schedule an initial visit so you can meet the staff, check the cleanliness, and evaluate the overall vibe.

The best time to find a vet is *before* you even bring baby Fido home, as you'll want to get your pup checked within the first 48 hours. Since vets are busy, go ahead and schedule that first appointment as far in advance as possible.

WHAT TO EXPECT AT YOUR FIRST VET VISIT

At your puppy's first wellness visit, your vet will:

- Pop your pooch onto the scale to check his weight
- Take your puppy's temperature
- Listen to his chest (*heart/lungs*) with a stethoscope

- Examine his eyes, ears, nose, teeth, paws, skin, coat, and genitalia by performing a full physical exam
- Test a fresh stool sample for parasites. It's not uncommon for puppies to have worms and vets to give a deworming treatment.
- Answer any medical or feeding questions you may have

- Go over future medical needs, such as parasite prevention, vaccinations, spay or neuter surgery, and microchipping
- Direct you to trusted groomers, trainers, or other resources based on your specific questions

PARASITES

Puppies are susceptible to both external and internal parasites.

External Parasites

Fleas—Fleas are very small, wingless insects that can jump up to eight inches high. They have four life stages: egg, larva, pupa, and adult. Once fleas leave their cocoons and become adults, they look for a warm-blooded host (*i.e. your pet*) to feed off. Shortly after their first blood meal, fleas breed and begin laying eggs in your pet's fur. Here's another scary fact: An adult female can lay about 40 eggs per day. Once those eggs mature into adults, they continue feeding off your dog and reproducing.

Adult fleas can consume as much as 15 times their weight in blood each day. If fleas suck too much of your dog's blood, your pooch could develop anemia (*a low red blood cell count*). Plus, along with blood meals, when a flea bites, it deposits a small amount of saliva under your pup's skin. Some dogs develop an allergy to this saliva, resulting in severe itching and skin irritation. Additionally, your dog could become infected with tapeworms if he ingests an infected flea. Along with intense itching around the anus, you may be able to see the tapeworms around your dog's anus or in his feces. Their appearance resembles a grain of rice.

Talk to your vet about the best flea treatment option for your pup. If you find fleas on your dog, your vet can also help you come up with the best treatment plan, which may include a special shampoo and medicated treatment. It can take one to three months, on average, to eliminate an infestation.

Ticks—Ticks are related to spiders, scorpions, and mites. They don't jump, fly, or drop from trees. They're patient little stalkers. Instead, they hide in low places, like brush, bushes, or in the grass. Normally, they sit and wait for an unsuspecting host to walk by, so they can grab on and hitch a ride. They start low and stroll to their feeding destination. During this blood meal, an infected tick has the potential to transmit an assortment of bacterial, protozoan, and viral pathogens—some of which can be deadly.

The number one way to prevent any tick-borne disease is to limit exposure to ticks. If there is a higher risk of transmission, tick preventatives can be purchased at the pet store, online, or your vet's office. It's important to ask your vet what's most common in your area, as ticks are much worse in certain places, like the northeastern states.

Internal Parasites

Worms—As I mentioned a few minutes ago, it's not uncommon for new puppies to come home with worms, specifically roundworms. Their appearance resembles spaghetti. A broad-spectrum dewormer can help rid your puppy's intestinal tract of various types of worms, and often your puppy will require multiple deworming treatments over the next few visits to eliminate them completely. Your vet will know what's best for your puppy.

Heartworm—Heartworm disease is caused by a parasitic worm, *Dirofilaria immitis*. These worms set up home in a dog's heart, lungs, and blood vessels, where they can cause devastating effects.

Heartworm disease is transmitted through an infected mosquito's bite. As they feast on a blood meal, they can pass infective larvae into the dog. It takes infective larvae six months to mature into adult worms, which resemble long, thin, cooked strands of spaghetti and can grow to 12" long. They have a lifespan between five to seven years. And get this: An infected dog can have anywhere from 1 to 250 worms living inside of him. As the population of worms increases and begins to infest the heart and lungs, you may notice:

- Chronic cough
- Shortness of breath
- Exercise intolerance
- Decreased appetite
- Weight loss
- Weakness/collapse

If untreated, the worm population will continue to increase. This is a potentially deadly disease, as the worms can cause blockages and damage to the heart, lungs, blood vessels, kidneys, liver, and other organs. Prevention is recommended for all dogs, 12 months a year. It comes in oral, topical, or injectable forms. You and your veterinarian will decide what's best for your dog.

Giardia—Giardia is a microscopic single-celled parasite that sets up house in the intestinal tract of its host. There, the parasites multiply and eventually become cysts. These cysts are infectious, shed through feces, and can survive in the environment for several weeks.

Dogs can become infected with Giardia if they swallow the cysts, most commonly by drinking contaminated water. Your pooch could also become infected by eating grass or anything else, like balls or toys, that have come in contact with infected poop.

Symptoms may include:

- Diarrhea
- Gas
- Vomiting
- Dehydration
- Weakness
- Loss of appetite
- Weight loss
- Foul-smelling stool

If your dog is diagnosed with Giardia, your vet will prescribe medication. Make sure to give it as ordered and on time. This is essential! Giardia can be challenging to treat, and it's not uncommon for dogs to need a second, and possibly even a third, round of medication.

CORE AND NON-CORE VACCINES

Getting your dog the proper vaccinations is one of the most important things you can do to keep your furbaby healthy. With that said, there are a wide variety of vaccines available and your puppy likely doesn't need them all. That's why vaccines are broken down into two categories: core and non-core.

Core vaccines are considered important for all dogs to get because all dogs are at risk for these diseases.

Canine Parvovirus—Often called parvo, canine parvovirus is a highly contagious and life-threatening virus that affects the stomach and small intestines. Once a dog has contracted parvo, the virus replicates. This takes place in the small intestine and can cause acute gastrointestinal problems as it destroys the digestive lining. This damage leads to severe dehydration. Additionally, it can affect a dog's bone marrow, cause a low white blood cell count *(these are the cells that fight off infection)*, and can lead to various heart complications.

The incubation period *(AKA the time between exposure and onset of symptoms)* is around three to seven days. Common warning signs and symptoms include:

- Decrease or loss of appetite
- Lethargy
- Depression
- Diarrhea *(normally bloody)*
- Vomiting
- High fever
- Many adult dogs show no symptoms at all

While any dog can get parvo, young puppies between six weeks and six months old, immuno-suppressed dogs, and unvaccinated dogs are at the greatest risk. One of the most important things to stress is how contagious this virus really is. Here's a crazy fact: It was first identified in the 1970s and only took two years to spread globally!

There is no cure for parvo. Vets focus on supportive care and treating symptoms. The majority of dogs require hospitalization in order to survive the virus. Some require stays as long as 7 to 14 days when they're severely ill. The hospitalization cost can be anywhere from $1,500-5,000, depending on the length of stay.

Distemper—Canine distemper is very contagious and another potentially deadly viral disease that attacks the respiratory, gastrointestinal, and nervous systems. Like parvo, the scariest part about canine distemper: There's no cure. Dogs can get distemper through direct contact with an infected animal or object. This virus is airborne. So, if an infected dog or animal coughs, sneezes, or barks, aerosol droplets are spread into the air, putting nearby dogs at risk. Pregnant mother dogs can also pass the virus to her puppies through the placenta.

Distemper-infected dogs experience a wide range of symptoms. Typically, the first symptom is watery/pus-like discharge coming from the eyes. Other symptoms:

- Fever
- Nasal discharge
- Loss of appetite
- Lethargy

- Coughing
- Vomiting
- Diarrhea

As the virus attacks the nervous system, infected dogs can also develop neurological symptoms, such as:

- Circling behavior
- Head tilt
- Muscle twitches
- Repetitive eye movements
- Convulsions with increased salivation and chewing motions
- Seizures
- Partial or complete paralysis

Dogs that survive usually suffer permanent damage to their nervous system. Puppies younger than four months old and unvaccinated dogs are at the highest risk.

Canine Hepatitis (Adenovirus)—Infectious canine hepatitis is a highly contagious viral disease caused by canine adenovirus type 1 (AKA CAV-1). Dogs can get the disease by inhaling or ingesting an infected animal's body fluids, such as urine, feces, blood, saliva, and nasal or eye secretions.

Once introduced into the body, the virus moves to the tonsils and then the bloodstream, where it can infect the eyes, liver, spleen, and kidneys within a few days. Puppies and unvaccinated dogs are at the highest risk.

Prevention for CAV-1 in dogs is done by giving the CAV-2 vaccine. You may be wondering, "What is CAV-2?" CAV-2 is a common adenovirus that causes respiratory illnesses, such as kennel cough. Since

CAV-2 offers a cross-immunity for CAV-1, the CAV-2 vaccine has become a standard part of the core vaccine protocol for preventing infectious canine hepatitis.

Rabies—This is a devastating viral disease that affects the central nervous system of all mammals, including dogs, cats, and people. It often results in death. Since rabid animals secrete the virus through their saliva, rabies is primarily passed to dogs through an infected animal's bite. In North America, the raccoon, skunk, fox, coyote, and bat are all top sources of infection.

After a bite occurs, the rabies virus travels through the nerves and spinal cord to the brain. Once the brain is infected, the virus multiplies and spreads to the salivary glands.

The incubation period can last weeks or even months, but, once your dog begins to show symptoms, they progress rapidly. Symptoms develop in one of two forms: the furious form or the paralytic ("dumb") form. Dogs can also experience a combination of the two.

Furious Form—Just like the name implies, this form is characterized by extreme behavioral changes. Once friendly and calm dogs become irritable and aggressive.

Paralytic Form—Just like the name implies, this form is characterized by weakness and paralysis. Dogs often experience excess saliva and an inability to swallow.

Once clinical signs appear, death usually occurs in less than a week.

There is no treatment for rabies in dogs. If you suspect your dog has rabies, call your vet immediately, as your dog will need to be quarantined and monitored. Oftentimes, the local animal control branch will get involved too. Vaccination is the way to prevent this illness. If your pet ever contacts a suspected rabid animal, your vet will booster the vaccine to improve immunity.

Rabies is a zoonotic disease, which means it can be transmitted to humans. Since it's a devastating virus, difficult to diagnose, and there is no treatment, in the United States, the rabies vaccination is mandatory by law. While boosters are required, the frequency depends on each state. Here's an interesting fact: The one-year and three-year rabies vaccinations *(volume and potency)* are the same. The only difference is the labeling and what the vet marks on the certificate required by law. Again, each state is different as to what time frame is legally acceptable.

Non-core vaccines are administered based on a dog's risk of exposure.

Bordetella—*Bordetella bronchiseptica* is a bacterium known to cause kennel cough in dogs. Since it's airborne, dogs can catch it just as you would catch a cold or the flu. Dogs that go to boarding facilities, daycares, grooming shops, and parks are considered high risk since they're in close contact with other dogs.

With kennel cough, symptoms usually appear in 5 to 10 days after exposure and can last up to three weeks. Perhaps the most distinctive symptom is a loud, dry, hacking cough. Others include a runny nose, sneezing, loss of appetite, tiredness, and fever.

Many dogs recover without treatment, but vets will work with pet parents to determine what's best for each individual dog. Both injectable and intranasal vaccines are available. Vaccinated dogs can still become infected, but it tends to be less severe and dogs recover quicker.

Canine Influenza Virus—The canine influenza virus—*more commonly referred to as the dog flu*—is a highly contagious virus that causes a respiratory infection in dogs. The majority of dogs exposed will develop mild symptoms, including coughing, sneezing, nasal discharge, lethargy, and loss of appetite. However, the first United States outbreak in Chicago showed some dogs developing severe cases with a high fever and clinical signs of pneumonia, requiring hospitalization.

Dogs who are around a lot of other dogs are considered a higher risk. While there is no known cure, veterinarians work to control symptoms and prevent secondary infection. Most dogs recover at home with proper care.

Leptospirosis—Often referred to as lepto, leptospirosis is an infectious disease that can affect both humans and animals, including our canine companions. It's caused by spiral-shaped bacteria called *leptospires*. If your dog becomes infected *(either by drinking contaminated water or coming into contact with an infected animal's urine)*, the bacteria can multiply in their bloodstream and eventually move into the tissues. They concentrate in the liver and kidneys, causing damage to these organs. The amount of damage depends on each dog's immune system.

Dogs can recover from mild infections. However, damage done can lead to liver failure and/or kidney failure. In these severe cases, the damage is often irreversible and quickly becomes fatal.

Signs vary from dog to dog, and younger animals with less developed immune systems are generally more seriously affected than older animals. But, common warning signs and symptoms include:

- Lethargy and severe weakness
- Sore muscles and stiffness

- Fever
- Vomiting
- Diarrhea
- Abdominal discomfort
- Refusal to eat
- Weight loss
- Depression
- Jaundice
- Acute renal failure
- Blood in the urine may occur
- Respiratory distress

Lepto is a zoonotic disease. Since people can contract Lepto through a dog's bodily fluids, it's essential to practice proper hygiene.

- Wear latex gloves when cleaning up after your dog
- If you are cleaning potentially contaminated surfaces, use an antibacterial cleaning solution or a solution of 1 part household bleach in 10 parts water
- Wash your hands regularly
- Avoid doggy kisses

Borrelia burgdorferi *(Lyme Disease)* — Lyme Disease is a tick-borne infection caused by the bacteria *Borrelia burgdorferi*. It's the most common form of tick-borne illness in the U.S. To transmit Lyme Disease, a tick must remain attached to its host for approximately 24 to 48 hours. That's why, if you're diligent and check your pooch *(and yourself)* after every outing, there's a better chance of spotting the unwanted hitchhiker. Then, you can grab a pair of tweezers or tick remover to get it off before it has a chance to transmit the disease. If you're uncomfortable removing the tick yourself, many vets will remove it for you as a walk-in technician appointment.

In the United States, the deer tick is most commonly found in the northeast, northern central states, mid-Atlantic, and parts of the west coast.

PUPPY SHOT SCHEDULE

Your puppy's vaccination series will begin when he's approximately six weeks old, and puppy shots should be completed around 16 weeks of age. Work with your vet to determine the best schedule for your puppy, as many vets will space out vaccines in smaller patients to prevent reactions *(dogs <10 pounds)*. While your vet may recommend additional non-core vaccines based on your puppy's lifestyle and risk level, here is a basic puppy shot core vaccine schedule:

- 6–8 weeks: first DHPP shot *(combined core vaccines of distemper, hepatitis, parvovirus, and parainfluenza)*
  - *Can add in Bordetella between 8-10 weeks (non-core)*
- 10–12 weeks: second DHPP shot
- 12-14 weeks: third DHPP shot
  - *Can add in Lepto, Influenza, and Lyme between 12-14 weeks (non-core)*
- 14-16 weeks: fourth DHPP shot, Rabies shot
  - *Rabies is administered at 16 weeks of age*

WHAT ARE TITERS?

Once your puppy has completed his first round of puppy shots and one-year boosters, I'm a huge believer in titers. In case you aren't familiar with the term, a titer test is a blood test that checks the antibodies for a particular disease. After you get the results, you'll know whether or not a previous vaccine is still protecting your pup. This is a great way to prevent over-vaccinating. The only downside? Titer tests can be a bit pricey. But, in my opinion, they're totally worth it.

IMMEDIATE VACCINE SIDE EFFECTS

After a vaccine, your dog may feel more tired than usual, sore, not eat as much, experience a little bout of diarrhea, or even throw up. Your vet will go over side effects in greater detail during your visit. You can also ask your veterinarian for a Benadryl dosage, as this medication can help your pet feel better after vaccines. If your dog experiences any mild side effects, keep a close eye on him. Serious side effects warrant another trip to the vet.

Why Your Dog Shouldn't Get Vaccines on a Friday

There's a famous quote that says: *"Sometimes the most important lessons are the ones we end up learning the hard way."* Well, if you ask me, truer words have never been spoken. The advice I'm about to share with you, you'll likely never hear from anyone else. But, it's the result of a vet visit gone horribly wrong. My hope? By sharing this experience, I can help someone else avoid the horrible *(yet, easily avoidable)* mistake that I made.

Story Time

When it came time to book Gigi's latest rabies booster, the best day and time for my schedule was Friday evening, right before the office closed for the weekend. It was the easiest time for me to sneak away from work. So, that Friday at 4 p.m., we marched down to the office and Gigi took that needle in her leg like a champ. But, her chipper personality quickly changed.

When we got home, Gigi slept for a few hours, eventually ate dinner, and then threw up. *Okay…that can be an immediate side effect. One pile of puke didn't leave me overly worried.* She slipped into a deep sleep for the rest of the evening. When she woke up in the morning, though, she vomited three times in a row. Then, I saw her face. It was blowing up like a balloon! Her normal light pink eyes turned as red as a tomato. She was clearly having a severe reaction. My biggest worry? That it would spread to her throat and obstruct her airway.

I immediately called our vet. But—*oh yeah*—they're closed on the weekend. So, my husband and I quickly Googled nearby emergency vet offices and hopped in our car. Thankfully, two shots *(Benadryl + a steroid)* and about $350 later, her swelling started to go down. She recovered quickly, but we learned an important lesson that day: Never get the dogs vaccinated on a Friday.

Many vet offices are closed on the weekend. So, if your dog has any sort of reaction or issue that needs immediate attention then your only real option is to run down to your local emergency vet office. While you're there, expect to pay more. I've had to go to the emergency vet a few times—when living in Pennsylvania, Texas, and now South Carolina. It's always an expensive trip. This last time, we paid once when we first arrived *(their emergency room fee)* and then again as we were leaving *(for the vet's time and the shots)*.

Another, and even more important thing about the emergency vet: You don't have any relationship with them. While the vet certainly treated Gigi with patience and care—*and she was incredibly knowledgeable*—I'm a creature of habit and would have preferred to see *my* vet. My vet knows Gigi's history and I just feel more comfortable there. Perhaps you're the same way.

Try to Avoid Late Evening Appointments

I get it—when you're working at an office, sometimes evening appointments are the most convenient. It's easier to sneak away. But, if you book vaccines or procedures late in the day and Fido winds up having a reaction when you get home, you probably won't be able to reach your vet because their office will more than likely be closed.

The Best Times to Schedule an Appointment

For vaccines: Try to schedule your appointment early in the workweek *(Monday-Wednesday)* and early in the day. Of course, you'll want to keep an eye on your dog after his shots. If you can't work from home that day, or take a half-day, ask a family member or friend if they can watch your dog for a few hours while you're gone.

For surgeries: Most vets already schedule surgeries in the morning so the staff can monitor patients as they wake up from anesthesia. Many vet's offices also schedule surgeries on specific days of the week. My advice: Try your best to avoid Fridays.

SPAYING OR NEUTERING: WHAT TO EXPECT & POST-OP

Your dog having surgery is a scary thought. Sure, there are some procedures *(like spaying a female dog or neutering a male dog)* that have become so common, many tend to think of them as routine. But they still cause pet parents to worry. Whether you choose to spay or neuter your pup is between you and your vet. But, since these surgeries are very common for puppies, I wanted to include a brief section on this topic.

What is Spaying *(ovariohysterectomy)*

When a female dog is spayed, she's put under general anesthesia. While under anesthesia, the vet will make an incision just below her belly button, into the abdomen, and remove her reproductive tract: both ovaries and uterus. Then, the vet will stitch the incision closed—those stitches will eventually dissolve over a few months. The exposed skin will also be closed with either skin glue, stitches, or, in some cases, staples.

What is Neutering *(orchiectomy)*

As with spaying, when your male dog is neutered, he's put under general anesthesia. While under anesthesia, the vet will make an incision right in front of his scrotal sac and remove both testicles, leaving the sac intact. Then, the vet will stitch the incision closed – those stitches will eventually dissolve over a few months. The exposed skin will also be closed with either skin glue, stitches, or, in some cases, staples. Sometimes a male dog will have swelling of their scrotum after the procedure, so your vet will provide you with tips to prevent this from occurring.

When and Why Spay or Neuter?

Puppies are generally spayed or neutered between six and nine months old, but you should consult with your vet to determine what's best for your dog. With larger breed dogs, it's now recommended to perform this surgery when they're fully grown to improve their urinary tract and musculo-skeletal system.

Some of the main benefits of these surgeries are to prevent unplanned pregnancy (*an unspayed female dog will go into heat twice a year, starting at about six months old*), mammary cancer, life-threatening pyometra (*infected uterus*), testicular cancer, prostatic enlargement/infection, and more. As you can see, these surgeries can reduce certain health risks down the road.

Scheduling the Appointment

When scheduling the surgery, ask your vet about eating and drinking restrictions, drop off time, surgery time, what exactly your dog will undergo, and the waking up process (*more on this in a minute*). This is also a good time to discuss pain management. Request a basic copy of post-surgical instructions so you can prepare. In general, spaying is much more invasive than neutering, and little girls will need more downtime to recover than little boys.

Drop Off

Usually, your veterinary staff will schedule drop off for early in the morning (*around 7 or 8 a.m.*). However, your dog's surgery may not actually take place until a few hours later. Meanwhile, you're at home worrying and the surgery hasn't even started. They request such an early drop off for a few reasons:

- To ensure your dog doesn't eat or drink anything
- Perform another full physical exam to ensure there are no recent changes
- Run any necessary tests
- Many will give your dog an anti-nausea medication to reduce the risk of regurgitation under anesthesia
- Get the IV started

To alleviate your worries, ask your vet when your dog's procedure is scheduled to start. Also, ask the office staff to keep you updated when surgery begins and as soon as it's over. Vets like to say, "No news is good news." Surgery days can be busy for a vet, as they want to focus completely on their patients. They will always call once your pup is out of surgery and recovering.

Post Surgery

When surgery is over, your dog will be taken to the post-op area where he/she will be monitored very closely. The staff will keep your puppy warm, and he/she may continue to get some fluids via IV. Slowly, your puppy will wake up from the anesthesia over a few hours. Every dog is different.

The vet technicians try to get puppies to urinate before going home, but sometimes it doesn't happen as functions can be slowed after anesthesia. If your puppy doesn't pee, make sure he/she does at some point later that same day. Your pet may also develop diarrhea from the medications given, but it is often short, resolving within 12 to 24 hours. Notify your vet if you have any concerns.

Discharge

Take someone with you when you pick up your pooch. This way, they can keep their eyes on the road while you keep your eyes on your pup. Don't be surprised if your dog is still groggy from the anesthesia and somewhat whiny. It'll likely be up to 24 hours before the full effects of anesthesia wear off. This is a good thing, though, because rest and quiet time are key.

As far as pain medications, your vet will have already medicated your pup. Your vet will also send you home with additional pain meds for the next few days. Depending on the circumstances, you may go home with an anti-inflammatory medication, sedative or relaxant medication, and maybe even an antibiotic. The vet will decide what's best for your dog.

Home

When you arrive home, immediately get your pup settled in a safe and comfortable space.

During the next few days (and even next few weeks), you'll need to keep a close eye on the incision. The suture line should appear clean. While there may be some redness and a small amount of clear to bloody/liquidy seepage the day of surgery, there should never be a lot of odorous or purulent drainage from the incision line, excessive bruising, swelling, or any open areas. Notify your vet immediately if you notice changes.

Never allow your dog to lick or gnaw at the incision. Most vets will send your dog home with a cone collar (there is also clothing you can put on your pup if he/she isn't tolerating the cone well). Again, the goal here is to prevent your pooch from licking or chewing at the incision. It's natural for your dog to try and lick the wound, but the last thing you want is for your dog to accidentally pull out his/her stitches and disturb the healing process. Your vet will tell you how long to keep the collar on, but it's usually for about 10 to 14 days.

Keep Your Pup Warm

As I mentioned a minute ago, anesthesia can take approximately 12 to 24 hours to clear out of your dog's system. During this period, he/she won't be able to regulate body temperature normally. So, it's important to keep your pup warm enough. You don't want to overheat him/her, just offer blankets and monitor closely so your dog doesn't get chilled.

Feeding

If you've ever had surgery, you know you can feel a bit nauseous after having anesthesia. So, go slow with the food. While your vet will give you formal feeding guidelines, she'll probably tell you to feed 1/4 to 1/2 the normal serving the night of surgery. Even if your pup is feeling good enough to eat … go slow.

Daily Activity While Recuperating

The best thing for a quick and uneventful recovery is rest. Just like with people, the more your pup rests, the quicker things can knit themselves back together and heal. Limiting activity is a little easier during the first couple of days, but, once your pup starts feeling better, he/she will want to get back to business. It's your job to keep your pup calm. Maybe you can have some lazy days and just watch television. I know my pooches love when I lazy around—they'll stay in bed with me all day.

Make Sure There is NO:

- Jumping onto or off of the couch
- Jumping onto or off of the bed
- Running up or down the stairs
- Activity of any kind that will put a strain on the incision! An open incision can quickly escalate and become a medical emergency.
- Playing around with other dogs or pets for up to two weeks
- Running off-leash
- Walking with extendable leashes
- Bathing the dog for at least 10 days

About Walks

Keep bathroom walks brief and use a short leash. At no time should your dog run free, even if it's only in your backyard. To limit exposure to extra contaminants, walk your dog in the cleanest area you can find (*where not too many other dogs relieve themselves*). This is especially important for small dogs whose bellies aren't too far off the ground. You have no idea what bacteria and parasites are lurking on that grass, which can brush against his/her wound. The last thing you want is an infection. If you have a private backyard, that's the best. But remember…on a short leash.

Microchips

When scheduling your dog's spay or neuter surgery, talk to your vet about microchips. A microchip is a small, rice-sized electronic chip that's implanted under a dog's skin, between his shoulder blades at the back of his neck. It isn't a GPS. Rather, it contains a unique tracking number that's registered to a database and linked to an account with the animal's info and pet parent's contact details.

If your dog goes missing and someone brings him to a shelter or veterinary clinic, one of the first things they'll do is wave a scanner over the dog's neck to check for a microchip. As long as the microchip registry has accurate and up-to-date information, the shelter or vet team can quickly find and contact the animal's family.

Not only do my dogs have microchips, but I've also seen their magic in action. Rewind the clock to when I was a television news reporter. After moving to Texas and starting fresh at a new station, the first story I covered was a family reunited with their dog after he went missing for several years. It was all thanks to the dog's microchip!

Your vet will likely implant your pup's microchip during their spay or neuter surgery. Then, it's up to you to keep your contact details up-to-date. It's good to check your pup's chip info once a year.

ARE ANNUAL VET VISITS WORTH IT?

Just like we see our primary care doctors once a year for a physical exam, it's recommended our canine companions see their doctors (*AKA the vet*) once a year for a check-up (*or twice a year for seniors, >7 years of age*).

I know a lot of pet parents question: *"But my dog is healthy. Do I really need to waste money on an annual check-up?"* If your budget allows, annual exams really are worth it because preventative healthcare can help prolong your dog's life!

During your dog's annual exam, your vet will:

- Ask a lot of questions about diet, eating habits, drinking habits, eliminating patterns, exercise, behavior, lifestyle, and general health. Something that may seem normal to you may serve as a red flag to your veterinarian based on health history.
- Examine your dog from snout to tail. This includes taking your pup's temperature, listening to his heart and lungs with a stethoscope, conducting an eye exam, checking his ears, checking his teeth, feeling all over the body to make sure there aren't any abnormalities, and more.
- Blood work—Your vet will likely run a Complete Blood Count (CBC), which is a count and examination of red blood cells, white blood cells, and platelets. Red blood cells are responsible for carrying oxygen. White blood cells play a key role in immunity. Platelets are required for

blood clotting. Additionally, they'll run a series of blood chemistries such as glucose, electrolytes, protein, cholesterol, thyroid, liver, kidney function, etc., to ensure your dog's organs and systems are functioning properly. It's very similar to what we have done at our yearly check-up.

- Stool sample—Your vet will likely ask you to bring a fresh stool sample for the lab to microscopically evaluate, ensuring there are no parasites. You would be surprised how many dogs do not show outward clinical signs of a parasitic infection right away.
- Urine sample—Your vet *may* ask you to bring a urine sample to check your pup's kidneys and urinary health. This is most important in seniors or dogs with prior urinary issues.
- Your vet *may* recommend additional testing during the wellness exam, depending on your dog's unique needs.

By thoroughly checking your dog's health, and updating their health records each year, it gives you and your vet a baseline of your dog's health status. Knowing what is normal is key to recognizing anything that may change or become abnormal. These regular check-ups can help you uncover a disease or condition before your dog ever shows signs of illness. Early detection can make a huge difference in prognosis, treatment, recovery, and cost!

PET INSURANCE & MEDICAL BILLS

Take it from someone who has raised dogs for decades, vet bills can be really expensive. Just like we enroll in health insurance plans to help cover our medical costs, there are also pet insurance plans. The best time to enroll? When your furkid is still a puppy! The younger your pup, the better your rates. As you shop around for the best plans, keep in mind some cover both emergency and routine vet visits, while others only cover emergency care.

Also, before selecting a plan, find out what conditions and treatments it covers. Read the fine print! If you have any questions or concerns, ask your vet for recommendations. Among the most popular providers are HealthyPaws, Nationwide, and Trupanion.

No insurance and hit with a hefty bill? CareCredit and Scratchpay are two payment plan options that let pet parents pay for medical bills over time.

VET RECORDS KEEPER

With so many life demands, it can be hard to remember what the heck we ate for breakfast, let alone all of our pup's medical details. That's why I recommend having a basic records keeper to jot down notes. Use the next few pages to help stay organized.

Pet Info

NAME:

DOB:

BREED:

FUR TYPE:

COLOR:

WEIGHT:

OWNER NAME:

PHONE:

ADDRESS:

EMERGENCY CONTACT:

EC PHONE:

VETERINARIAN:

VET PHONE:

VET ADDRESS:

PET INSURANCE:

POLICY #:

MICROCHIP ID #:

RABIES #:

MEDICAL CONDITIONS:

ALLERGIES:

Monthly Meds

NAME: DOB:

HEARTWORM

JAN: FEB: MAR: APR: MAY: JUN: JUL: AUG: SEPT: OCT: NOV: DEC:

FLEA & TICK

JAN: FEB: MAR: APR: MAY: JUN: JUL: AUG: SEPT: OCT: NOV: DEC:

OTHER

JAN: FEB: MAR: APR: MAY: JUN: JUL: AUG: SEPT: OCT: NOV: DEC:

OTHER

JAN: FEB: MAR: APR: MAY: JUN: JUL: AUG: SEPT: OCT: NOV: DEC:

OTHER

JAN: FEB: MAR: APR: MAY: JUN: JUL: AUG: SEPT: OCT: NOV: DEC:

Vet Records

NAME:

DOB:

VACCINATIONS:

TYPE:

DATE:

LABS:

SURGERY:

Pet Notes

DIY Pet First Aid Kit

While we're chatting about canine wellness, consider putting together your own pet first aid kit in case of an emergency or accident.

To put it simply: You never know when something bad is going to happen. Within the first few weeks of welcoming Gigi into my home, something horrible happened. I took her to the nearby tennis court to let her run around in an enclosed space when a big gust of wind came and knocked down the heavy gate. Apparently, the bolts were loose and the gate wasn't secure. I almost had a heart attack when I heard 4-pound Gigi shriek at the top of her lungs and run away from the fallen gate. It had landed on one of her paws, leaving a gash and lots of pain. As scary as that night was, fortunately, I had a pet first aid kit on hand and was able to tend to her on our way to the emergency vet.

Essentials

- Storage box with a snap-lock lid to house all of your supplies
- Gauze pads for covering open wounds and clotting
- Cotton balls and Q-tips for cleanup and topical application
- Antibiotic ointment for open wounds
- Liquid bandage formulated for pets for sealing open wounds
- Styptic powder to quickly clot bleeding nails
- Vet wraps for compression and splints
- Adhesive tape to secure bandages
- Blunt end scissors to cut bandage wraps and tape
- Regular tweezers and dog tick remover in case something is stuck on your dog's body
- 3% hydrogen peroxide to induce vomiting in case your dog eats something toxic *(always consult with a vet before attempting to induce vomiting)*
- Saline solution for eyes and rinsing
- Water bottle for rinsing wounds and hydration
- Oral syringe to administer medicine
- Ice/heat pack for sore muscles and bruises
- Disposable gloves to protect your hands
- Sanitizer to clean your hands after handling open wounds
- Towel for cleanup
- Small flashlight
- Vet records in case emergency personnel need to know your dog's medical history

ANIMAL POISON CONTROL

Along with your veterinarian, the ASPCA Animal Poison Control Center may serve as your go-to source for any animal poison-related emergencies. They're available through their hotline 24 hours a day, 365 days a year. If you think your pet may have ingested a potentially poisonous or toxic substance, give them a call at: (888) 426-4435. A consultation fee may apply.

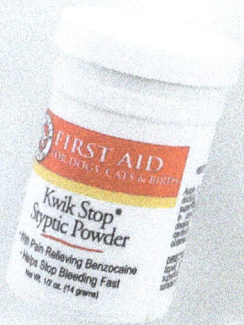

CHAPTER 9

Doggy Dining: What's on the Menu?

Just like newborn babies grow, develop, and mature at a pretty rapid speed, so do young puppies. It's amazing to watch their progress week after week. But as their teeth, bones, muscles, and organs continue to develop, one thing is clear: Puppies need sufficient nutrients to help them thrive. With that said, deciding what (and how) to feed your new puppy can feel overwhelming. *I've been there!*

Take a walk down the food aisles of your local pet store or do a simple Google search for 'dog food'

and you'll quickly realize there are so many choices. You may be wondering: *Should I feed kibble? Wet canned foods? Is fresh food worth the extra cost? Is puppy-formulated food all that different from adult dog food? How many times a day do I need to feed my puppy? Can I just let their food sit out all day, or do I need to portion out servings?*

Let's take a closer look, starting with how puppies eat from the time they're born, all the way up until they hit their first birthday.

PUPPY FEEDING TIMELINE

1–4 Weeks Old

During a puppy's first month of life, he'll ideally be snuggled up against his mommy and getting essential nutrients from her milk. A mother's milk provides everything her pups need to thrive within the first month of life. Generally, one-week-old new-born puppies nurse every two hours. As they grow and develop, the amount of time between each meal increases.

4–6 Weeks Old

Along with nursing momma's milk, once puppies reach four weeks of age, they're introduced to soft food. At this stage, puppies are generally given a combination of dry puppy kibble soaked in milk replacer and/or warm water. This mixture—referred to as gruel—is mashed or blended and then served.

After a puppy's first week on gruel, the amount of liquid is decreased. Eating a thicker version of this mush helps prepare them for the next phase: moistened solid food.

6–12 Weeks Old

Puppies begin weaning off momma's milk at about four weeks old, and they're completely weaned as of six to eight weeks. By this point, puppies are growing razor-sharp teeth. So, usually, breeders or caretakers will help transition the puppies from gruel to moistened solid food, and then to straight dry kibble.

Since growing puppies require more calories, protein, fat, and other essential nutrients per pound than adult dogs, they need food formulated for their current life stage. We'll talk more about this in a minute.

At this age, puppies are generally eating four times a day.

3–6 Months Old

Ideally, puppies will stay with their mother and lit-termates until they're about 8 to 12 weeks old. So, when you bring your puppy home, he should already have a solid food routine. Find out what your puppy is used to eating and stick with that for at least a week or two, while your puppy gets used to his new home. *Note: Abrupt food changes can lead to upset stomach and diarrhea. Instead, gradually replace your pup's old food with his new food over 7 to 10 days.*

Regardless of brand, puppies should eat three times a day. This is a pretty easy schedule to follow since you can match it up to your own breakfast, lunch, and dinner times. Smaller meals are easier for puppies to digest, can help keep their energy levels steady, and help prevent obesity.

During this feeding stage, you should notice your puppy's little round potbelly start to disappear.

6 Months Old and Up

At this point, you can transition your puppy to twice-daily feeding. Twice-daily or once-daily is the schedule you'll stick with all through adulthood.

IMPORTANT NUTRIENTS THAT SET PUPPY FOOD APART

Puppies have different nutritional needs than adult and senior dogs, and they're at risk of deficiencies if they don't eat a diet that considers their needs.

Protein—Growing puppies need more protein, as it plays a vital role in growth and development. When selecting the perfect food for your puppy, keep this in mind: The highest-quality source of protein is always animal protein versus plant protein.

Fats—Incorporating the right kind, and ratio, of healthy fats is essential for developing puppies.

The fat conversation usually surrounds Omega-3s and Omega-6s. Without getting too in-depth, docosahexaenoic acid (DHA)—which is a type of Omega-3—is a particularly important element for a growing pup. The best sources of DHA are fish, such as sardines.

Calcium & Phosphorus—Calcium and phosphorus are responsible for a variety of essential bodily functions and, as such, are an incredibly important part of a puppy's nutritional needs.

LARGE BREED PUPPIES

Large breed puppies should take longer to grow than small breeds and, as a result, their food needs extra consideration. Studies show that large breed puppies who grow too quickly are at risk of developing orthopedic diseases and obesity. There are foods formulated for large breed puppies, which are slightly lower in fat, calcium, and phosphorus.

CHOOSING THE RIGHT LIFE STAGE FOOD

The Association of American Feed Control Officials (AAFCO) is the organization that sets standards for pet food—including nutrient ratios, ingredient allowances, and the terminology allowed on packaging.

When shopping for puppy food, look at bags marked as either *Puppy* or *All Life Stages*. Foods designed for *All Life Stages* means they meet AAFCO's standards for both growth and maintenance. In other words, it has everything your maturing puppy needs to thrive and you won't have to transition to a new food once young Fido graduates to adulthood.

DON'T FALL FOR THESE DOG FOOD MARKETING TRICKS

As a dog food newbie, it's important to learn the land of labels. Dog food labels can be incredibly misleading and are often filled with buzzwords that make pet parents feel like certain foods are way healthier than they really are. Here are some important things to keep in mind when shopping for dog food:

First Ingredient *(It's Not Always as Impressive as You Think)*—AAFCO requires food manufacturers to list ingredients in order of weight. So, naturally, you may think the first ingredient is the most prominent. But, not so fast! These labels are created *before* the product is cooked and processed. Since meat holds a lot of water, it weighs significantly more before cooking. So, if you spot a food label that lists meat first and then various grains as the second, third, and fourth ingredients, there may actually be more grain in the food than meat.

Ingredient Splitting *(Beware)*—Another common way marketers sneak meat into that #1 spot is by dividing up ingredients. For example, you may find a label that looks like this: chicken, chicken meal, brown rice, white rice, rice gluten, rice bran, split peas, pea protein, potato, potato starch. But that same label could also look like this: rice, peas, chicken, potatoes. That second version isn't as appealing, right?

Ingredient Lingo *(Useless Buzzwords)*—If a dog food bag shows photos of healthy chunks of meat and fresh vegetables on the cover, that doesn't necessarily mean those ingredients are packed inside. Some buzzwords to watch for:

- Foods labeled with the words "Dinner," "Nugget," or "Formula" only have to contain 25% actual meat.
- Foods labeled "with chicken," "with beef," or "with" any other protein only have to contain 3% meat.
- "Flavor" is perhaps the worst term. Dog food bags labeled with the word "Flavor" don't have to contain any real meat at all.

Natural *(Whatever That Means)*—Consumers love the word "Natural." But, when it comes to pet food, this word isn't very meaningful.

Complete *(But What About Quality?)*—You'll often see the words "Complete and Balanced" on pet foods. But, what the heck does that mean? According to AAFCO, the term "complete" means the product contains all of the nutrients it's supposed to. But that doesn't necessarily mean those nutrients come from quality sources. As the pet parent, it's up to you to dig a little deeper.

A FEW RED-FLAG INGREDIENTS TO AVOID

Before buying pet food, make sure to flip the bag over and take a peek at the ingredient label. You don't want to catch any of these names on that list:

Dangerous Preservatives—Butylated-hydroxyanisole (BHA), Butylated Hydroxytoluene (BHT), Ethoxyquin, Propylene Glycol

Cheap Fillers—Wheat, corn, soy

Other Red Flag Ingredients—Animal by-products, nondescript fats (*i.e. animal fat*), high-fructose corn syrup, corn syrup, Monosodium Glutamate (MSG), artificial flavors, artificial colors/food dyes

Kibble Storage

If you plan to feed your dog kibble, always check expiration dates (*choose a bag that has the latest date*) and opt for smaller bags (*ones you can use up in less than a month*). I know large bags may seem more cost-effective when looking at the unit price, but, the expiration date listed on a bag of kibble only counts toward a bag that's sealed and intact. So, once the bag is opened, the expiration date is no longer accurate.

As soon as you open the bag, air and oxygen hit the kibble and the oxidation process begins. Oxidation is where a chain of chemical reactions oxidizes the fats and turns them rancid. As fats in (*and sprayed on*) kibble turn rancid, the nutritional value decreases. So, if your dog continues to eat this food, his tummy may get full, but he won't get the nourishment you had intended. Additionally, long-term consumption of rancid fats can make your dog sick.

In general, rancid fats have a distinct smell. Many describe it as a plastic odor. The best thing you can do is get familiar with how a fresh bag smells when you bring it home so you'll know what it should smell like. I must admit, I've never smelled a bag of kibble that made me say, "*Yum.*" But, I'm familiar with what's normal and what it's supposed to smell like when it's freshly opened. It's also a good idea to inspect the kibble for anything that looks off-color, moldy, or you would consider abnormal. Keep an eye on your dog's stools and be aware that spoiled food may cause diarrhea.

As far as proper storage goes, the original bag is designed specifically to help keep kibble fresh for as long as possible, and to safeguard it from the effects of moisture and oxygen. Higher quality kibbles use higher-quality bags in their packaging. Never leave the bag open to the air. Instead, roll or fold down the top of the bag, while pressing out as much air as you can. Use a clip to secure it closed. Remember: In the case of kibble storage, the goal is to keep the air and moisture out. Every time you open the bag, oxidation increases.

A lot of places sell plastic or tin containers, advertising them as a great way to store kibble. If you want to use one of these containers, that's fine. But there are some things to consider:

1. Make sure the container is airtight and food-grade.
2. Don't just pour the kibble into the container. Rather, keep the kibble in its original bag and then place the entire bag into the container. Why? Well, the fats from the kibble can seep into the plastic container's walls and contaminate the kibble as it's turning rancid.
3. Every time you change to a new kibble bag, thoroughly wash and dry the storage container, just in case there is any fat residue left on the walls. You don't want to risk contaminating a new bag of food.

Along with keeping kibble in its original bag, store it in a cool, dry place—preferably in the pantry. You never want to store your kibble in places like the garage or basement where the temperature and moisture are not as controlled. Kibble stored in a garage or basement is also more prone to contamination by rodents.

IS FRESH FOOD WORTH THE EXTRA COST?

If you feed your dog kibble then opt for the highest quality kibble you possible can *(keeping in mind the tips mentioned on the last few pages)*. But, if it's within your budget, fresh food that's been formulated and properly balanced by a vet nutritionist is the clear winner. And the earlier you start your puppy on fresh, the better. Filled with real meats and Fido-friendly veggies, fresh foods are considered the most species-appropriate for our canine companions. Transitioning from processed kibble to a fresh diet offers a lot of benefits:

Stronger Immune System & Less Risk of Certain Diseases—Diet plays a large role in many diseases, such as diabetes and even cancer. The sad reality is, the majority of processed kibbles are filled with questionable preservatives, cheap fillers, and red-flag ingredients. Fresh food offers better nutrition, which is the clearest path to a healthier and longer life!

More Energy—Overly processed diets can be hard for a dog's digestive system to fully break down. That means they may not fully absorb and benefit from the nutrients inside. So, in essence, it goes in one end and out the other. That's not the case with fresh ingredients. With so many more nutrients being absorbed into their system, they're left fueled with energy.

Better Digestive Health—In general, dogs who are fed a fresh food diet will produce smaller poops because the food is being more effectively absorbed into their body. On the flip side, if your dog's food is filled with cheap fillers and excessive amounts of fiber, he may not properly absorb the nutrients from his meals. This will result in large and bulky stools.

Healthier Body Weight—Kibble is pretty easy to pour into a bowl and leave out for your dog to graze all day. Free-feeding can easily lead to overeating, which leaves your dog packing a few extra pounds. Instead, fresh meals are properly portioned out and quickly gobbled up!

Not as Thirsty—Dogs who eat dry kibble tend to become excessively thirsty and will likely need more water because of the lack of moisture in their food.

Healthier Skin and Shinier Coat—Fresh food is filled with essential fatty acids that nourish your dog's skin and transform their coat from dull to shiny.

If you choose to home-cook for your dog, consult with a canine nutritionist to ensure your meals are properly balanced. For peace of mind and convenience, there are plenty of reputable fresh food subscription services where meals are formulated by vet nutritionists and prepared with your dog in mind.

HOW MUCH SHOULD MY PUPPY EAT?

The answer to this question isn't so black and white. The amount of food your puppy needs will depend on a lot of factors, such as age, size, breed, and activity level. Plus, the type of food you've chosen to feed also matters.

If you're feeding dry kibble, you can reference the back of the bag to see how many cups or scoops are recommended. However, keep in mind this recommendation is relatively broad and leaves room for error. It's better to figure out how many calories your puppy needs, which you can determine with some help from your vet and online tools.

If you're feeding fresh food from a subscription service then—good news—the company will do this work for you! You simply fill out an online form, sharing your dog's breed, current weight, goal weight, age, lifestyle, and eating habits. Then, based on your answers, the company will calculate how many calories your dog should eat each day.

Most importantly, always keep an eye on your dog's body shape to determine if he's underweight, ideal, or overweight.

How to Tell if Your Dog Is a Healthy Body Weight

Maintaining a healthy weight is essential for your dog's overall health and well-being. Obesity in dogs is linked to many health problems:

- Heart Disease
- High Blood Pressure
- Respiratory Disease
- Diabetes
- Certain Cancers
- Arthritis
- Heat Intolerance
- Reproductive Issues
- Decreased Energy
- Depression
- Decreased Quality of Life
- Decreased Lifespan

Along with plopping your pooch onto the scale at your vet's office to see if he weighs within a healthy range for his specific breed, you can also get an idea by simply looking at your pup's overall body shape and feeling for his bones.

Signs Your Dog Is Too Thin/Underweight

- Ribcage is highly visible
- Spine clearly sticks out
- Hip bones clearly stick out
- Very little fat cover or padding between the skin and bones
- Dramatic waist cinch when viewed from above
- Dramatic abdominal tuck when viewed from the side

Signs Your Dog Is an Ideal Weight

- Ribs can be felt, but not easily seen
- Waist slightly cinches when viewed from above
- Abs tuck up when viewed from the side

Signs Your Dog Is Overweight/Obese

- Ribs are not visible and, when feeling for the ribs, you'll notice thicker padding above them
- Waist is barely visible or even bulges out when viewed from above
- Belly may look round and fall to either the same level as the chest or even further to the ground than the chest when viewed from the side
- Fat deposits and skin folds develop near the base of the tail, back, and neck

WATCH THE TREATS

To help your dog maintain an ideal weight, watch how many treats you give young Fido! Treats are easily doled out by the dozen during training sessions and other reward-worthy moments. But, make sure each bite is teeny tiny, to avoid a caloric buildup.

Unfortunately, I can't tell you the exact number of treats you should give your dog in a day. The number that's appropriate for my 6-pound Chihuahua is very different from someone's 130-pound Great Dane. Plus, a lap-dog who snoozes all day won't be able to have quite as many snacks as an active dog. Just like with food portions, how many treats a dog can eat depends on their size, activity level, age, and health status. *Makes sense, right?*

My Personal Philosophy

In general, if you're feeding one healthy mid-day treat and a couple of small, tasty bites during training/enrichment sessions then your pup's treat intake is likely just fine.

I personally offer my toy poodle and Chihuahua between three or four treats throughout the day. When they train or play with puzzle toys, I break one biscuit into a lot of super teeny tiny pieces, so they think they're eating more. Since my furkids are small, I keep their treats small too. Through moderation, they're easily able to maintain ideal body weight.

The More Formal Guideline

If you ask your vet or canine nutritionist, they'll tell you treats should make up no more than 10% of your dog's total caloric intake. So, once you know the total number of calories your dog should eat in a day, do the math to calculate 10%. For example, if your dog can eat 500 calories a day then no more than 50 calories should come from treats. The other 450 would come from their meals.

If you've ever been on a diet then you know how quickly those calories add up. So, remain mindful of treats, table scraps, and any extra bites.

Remember: Treats are Treats *(Not Meals)*

Your dog's treats are equivalent to your afternoon snack or dessert. Dog treats are meant to taste yummy and excite your pup's taste buds, but they're not properly balanced to satisfy nutritional needs. If you feed a lot of treats then you'll need to adjust Fido's meals accordingly. But, keep in mind, if you consistently pull back on your pup's main meals to offer more treats then you run the risk of nutritional deficiencies.

Always Make Treats Healthy

While treats shouldn't be viewed as meals, I still urge pet parents to choose treats wisely and use snack-time as an extra way to nourish their dog's body with key nutrients. Just equate it to your own snack time. If you're going to consume calories for an afternoon snack, you're much better off eating celery sticks with a little peanut butter or a cup of fruit than a chocolate bar or bag of chips. Well, it's the same for our dogs. To ensure my dogs' treats are as healthy as possible, I personally prefer to make my own.

TOP 3 REASONS TO MAKE YOUR OWN DOG TREATS

Control Ingredients

Preservatives, cheap fillers, and food dyes…oh my! Have you ever read through the ingredient label of your store-bought dog treats? While some are definitely better than others, processed biscuits, jerky, and chews usually contain questionable ingredients that your dog is better off avoiding. This was something my family and I had no clue about until we had a couple of health scares and started digging into dog nutrition.

I look back at some of the snacks we used to feed our dogs and I just cringe. I remember as a little girl hopping into the car with my dad and driving down to this small-town pet shop to pick up dozens of rawhide bones. We couldn't wait to get home where we were greeted by a pack of happy dogs, anxiously waiting to sink their teeth into their tasty treat. Growing up, my dogs loved to slobber and chew on rawhides, and we never even thought to question whether they were healthy or not. We just assumed they were. But you know what they say about assuming.

Today we know rawhides are covered in chemicals, pose a choking risk, and are linked to intestinal blockages. My family found that last one out the hard way when, more than a decade ago, my mom's toy poodle, Tina, experienced intestinal bleeding from rawhides. Thankfully, little Tina survived and went on to live a long, happy life. But there are a lot of dogs out there who aren't that lucky. Needless to say, I don't feed my Diego and Gigi rawhides. My advice: Avoid them for your pup too!

That was health scare number one for my family. Number two happened when another family dog developed a kidney disorder as a direct result of eating treats manufactured in China.

Like processed foods, a big problem with many commercial snacks is their questionable ingredients. Dangerous preservatives and cheap fillers should be left out of your dog's diet. Artificial colorings are another thing to watch for. While they certainly make treats look pretty, fake coloring and food dyes have been linked to a rainbow of health risks in both humans and animals. Many manufacturers also add corn syrup and sugar to dog treats to make them more palatable. My jaw dropped when I saw sugar listed as an ingredient in my former-favorite chicken jerky strips. Just like how sugar affects humans, it can also contribute to obesity, diabetes, inflammation, and cancers in pets.

With homemade treats, you get to control everything that's included in your pup's snacks—from a particular ingredient to the quality of that ingredient.

Tailor to Your Dog's Dietary Needs

If your dog has a food intolerance or allergy, suffers from pancreatitis, or is diabetic then finding treats that fit Fido's dietary needs can be a daunting task. In certain cases, even if your dog isn't sensitive to a type of food, you may still want to avoid a particular ingredient because of your own dietary restrictions. If a puppy parent has Celiac disease, for example, they may want their pooch eating gluten-free just to keep their household free of the controversial sticky protein. By baking homemade treats, you can easily avoid any ingredient your heart desires.

May Save You Money

I don't know about your spending habits, but throughout my many years of buying commercial dog treats, dropping $100 or more during a trip to the pet store was not uncommon. While a bag of treats here and a few bones there may not seem like a lot of money when you reach the checkout counter, all of those dollars add up. I've easily spent thousands each year on *cheap* treats.

If you're someone who already bakes then, chances are, you have many tools and ingredients in your kitchen right now, meaning you can whip up custom treat creations without dropping a dime.

Recipe Time

Sprinkled across the next few pages, you'll find some of my favorite healthy dog treat recipes. From crunchy biscuits to a collection of protein-packed soft chews, these recipes were created right in my kitchen!

Before you bust out the baking equipment, here are a few important tips:

Measuring—When measuring flour, a lot of people have the urge to take their measuring cup, stick it in the flour bag, and scoop. Does that sound familiar? While it may be the easiest way to gather a cup of flour, it won't leave you with an accurate measurement. Instead, all of my recipes use the traditional spoon and level method.

1. Take a spoon and fluffy up the flour so it is no longer compacted in the bag or canister.
2. Spoon the flour into a dry measuring cup until it reaches the top. Do not compact it, tap it, or press it down. Just leave it fluffy.
3. Use the back of a knife to level off the flour.

Rolling Biscuit Dough: In all of my biscuit recipes, you'll notice I recommend sandwiching your dough ball between two pieces of parchment paper before rolling it out flat with a rolling pin. Here's what I do: I place a silicone baking mat on the countertop to create a non-slip grip. Next, I layer a piece of parchment paper, the dough ball, and another piece of parchment paper on top. Then, it's time to grab your rolling pin. This trick is a major lifesaver when working with either sticky doughs or drier doughs.

With that said, I use this method every time I roll a dog biscuit dough ball. Why? Well, there are a few reasons:

- Some bakers dust their work surface and rolling pin with flour before rolling out their dough to prevent the mixture from sticking. However, the parchment paper sandwich method eliminates the need to use extra flour. If you ask me, when you're working with rather expensive flours, like almond flour, it's a shame to waste even a bit.
- It keeps the rolling pin clean, meaning less cleanup for you.
- It keeps the dough surface smooth, which translates into prettier treats.

The Fido-Friendly Flours I Keep in My Pantry

- Almond flour
- Brown rice flour
- Buckwheat flour
- Coconut flour
- Garbanzo bean flour
- Oat flour
- Quinoa flour
- Tapioca flour

Peanut Butter Pumpkin Biscuits

Ingredients

- 3 cups brown rice flour
- 1 cup oat flour
- ¾ cup water
- ½ cup organic peanut butter
- ½ cup 100% pure pumpkin purée

Directions

1. Preheat the oven to 350°F and line two baking sheets with parchment paper. Set aside.
2. In a large mixing bowl, whisk together brown rice flour and oat flour.
3. Make a well in the center of your dry ingredients and add water, peanut butter, and pumpkin purée.
4. Mix everything together with a spoon until you're left with a crumbly mixture.
5. With your hands, knead the dough for several minutes, eventually forming a dough ball.
6. Sandwich dough ball in between two pieces of parchment paper. With a rolling pin, roll dough to about ¼" thick.
7. Using a cookie cutter, stamp out biscuits and place them on a baking sheet. While these treats won't spread, still leave a little room between each biscuit.
8. Bake for about 25–30 minutes, or until fully cooked.
9. Transfer to a wire rack to cool.

Notes

- When selecting a Fido-friendly peanut butter, check the ingredient label and make sure you don't see Xylitol listed. Xylitol is a sweetener that's toxic to dogs and found in some peanut butter.
- Store in an airtight container in the refrigerator for up to 2 weeks or in the freezer for up to 3 months.

> ▶ *See this recipe in action on youtube.com/prouddogmom*

Tropical Treasure Biscuits

Ingredients

- 2 cups oat flour
- ¼ cup coconut flour
- 1 large ripe banana
- 4 ounces fresh pineapple
- 2 tablespoons coconut oil

Directions

1. Preheat the oven to 350°F and line two baking sheets with parchment paper. Set aside.
2. In a large mixing bowl, whisk together oat flour and coconut flour. Set aside.
3. In a blender, add banana, pineapple, and coconut oil and blend until smooth.
4. Make a well in the center of your dry ingredients and add wet ingredients.
5. Mix everything together with a spoon until you're left with a crumbly mixture.
6. Using your hands, knead the dough for several minutes, eventually forming a dough ball. The dough may seem sticky after a minute or two, just keep kneading.
7. Sandwich dough ball in between two pieces of parchment paper. With a rolling pin, roll dough to about ¼" thick.
8. Using a cookie cutter, stamp out biscuits and place them on a baking sheet. While these treats won't spread, still leave a little room between each biscuit.
9. Bake for 25–30 minutes, or until fully cooked.
10. Transfer to a wire rack to cool.

Notes

- Don't use canned pineapple in place of fresh, as canned often contains syrup and added sugars that aren't healthy for dogs.
- Store in an airtight container in the refrigerator for up to 1 week or in the freezer for up to 1 month.

▶ *See this recipe in action on youtube.com/prouddogmom*

Quinoa Crunch

Ingredients

- 1½ cups quinoa flour
- ½ cup coconut flour
- 1 large egg
- ¼ cup 100% pure pumpkin purée
- 2 tablespoons coconut oil
- 2 tablespoons water

Directions

1. Preheat the oven to 325°F and line two baking sheets with parchment paper. Set aside.
2. In a large mixing bowl, whisk together quinoa flour and coconut flour.
3. Make a well in the center of your dry ingredients and add egg, pumpkin purée, coconut oil, and water.
4. Mix everything together with a spoon until you're left with a crumbly mixture.
5. With your hands, knead the dough for several minutes, eventually forming a dough ball. The dough will feel dry at first, just keep folding and kneading until you're left with a Play-doh-like consistency.
6. Sandwich dough ball in between two pieces of parchment paper. With a rolling pin, roll dough to about ¼" thick.
7. Using a cookie cutter, stamp out biscuits and place them on a baking sheet. While these treats won't spread, still leave a little room between each biscuit.
8. Bake for 25 minutes. Once the timer goes off, flip treats over and bake another 5 minutes.
9. Transfer to a wire rack to cool.

Notes:

- Store treats in an airtight container in the refrigerator for up to 2 weeks or in the freezer for up to 3 months.

See this recipe in action on youtube.com/prouddogmom

Doggy Meatballs

Ingredients

- 1 pound lean ground turkey
- ½ can sardines, (skinless, boneless, in water, no salt added)
- ½ cup super-fine almond flour
- 1 large egg

Directions

1. Preheat the oven to 350°F and line two baking sheets with parchment. (If using a large baking sheet then you may just need one.) Set aside.
2. Put all ingredients into a mixing bowl or KitchenAid and combine.
3. With your hands, form meat mixture into mini meatballs and place on the parchment paper-lined baking sheet.
4. Bake for 25–30 minutes. Bake time will be slightly different depending on the size of your meatballs. Just keep an eye on them!

Notes

- Before serving, I like to break my meatballs into small, bite-sized chunks, making it easier for my small dogs to eat.
- Once cooled, store doggy meatballs in an airtight container in the refrigerator for up to 3 days, or in the freezer for up to 1 month.

See this recipe in action on youtube.com/prouddogmom

Salmon and Veggie Muffins

Ingredients

- Coconut oil, for greasing
- 1 can salmon, (skinless, boneless, in water, no salt added)
- 3 broccoli florets
- 1 large egg
- ¼ cup garbanzo bean flour

Directions

1. Preheat the oven to 350°F and grease a mini-muffin tin with coconut oil. Set aside.
2. Drain canned salmon and dump into a medium-size mixing bowl. Set aside.
3. Using a food processor, pulse broccoli until you're left with extremely fine pieces. Be careful not to purée the veggie, though.
4. Add broccoli bits and remaining ingredients to the salmon and mix until thoroughly combined.
5. Spoon mixture into muffin tin.
6. Bake for 15 minutes, or until edges are lightly golden and fully set.
7. Let treats cool in muffin tin for about 5 minutes and then transfer to a wire rack to finish cooling.

Notes

- No broccoli? No problem! Swap for 1/4 cup finely chopped spinach, grated carrots, or grated zucchini.
- Before serving, I like to break my muffins into small, bite-sized chunks, making it easier for my small dogs to eat.
- Store in an airtight container in the refrigerator for up to 3 days or in the freezer for up to 1 month.

▶ *See this recipe in action on youtube.com/prouddogmom*

Sardine Fish Paws

Ingredients

- 1 can sardines, (skinless, boneless, in water, no salt added)
- 1 large egg
- ¼ teaspoon turmeric
- Pinch ground black pepper
- ¼ cup almond flour

Directions

1. Preheat the oven to 350°F.
2. Drain canned sardines well.
3. Add drained sardines, egg, turmeric, and ground black pepper into a food processor. Mix until you're left with a thick paste consistency.
4. Spoon mixture into a mixing bowl.
5. Add flour and mix in with a spoon.
6. Either form into little balls (like mini meatballs) and place on a parchment paper-lined baking sheet OR stuff into a silicone mold of your choice.
7. Bake for 15 minutes.
8. Let cool before serving to your drooling dogs.

Note

- As tempting as it may be to add the almond flour into the food processor along with the other ingredients, don't. The texture will come out too thin if you do.
- The pinch of ground black pepper will help your dog's body better absorb all of turmeric's goodness. If your pup is on medication, however, omit the pepper.
- Store in an airtight container in the refrigerator for up to 3 days or in the freezer for up to 1 month.

See this recipe in action on youtube.com/prouddogmom

Baked Liver Bites

Ingredients

- ¼ pound frozen beef liver

Directions

1. Line a baking sheet with parchment paper. Set aside for later.
2. While the beef liver is still frozen, place on a cutting board and use a sharp knife to cut into strips. Then, cut strips into bite-sized squares.
3. Let the frozen beef liver defrost on the cutting board–it will only take a few minutes. In the meantime, preheat the oven to 350°F.
4. Once the beef liver is defrosted, blot with a paper towel. I like to wear kitchen gloves for this part because defrosted beef liver is pretty bloody. Then, transfer to a parchment paper-lined baking sheet.
5. Bake for 30 minutes.
6. Let cool on the baking sheet before transferring to an airtight container for storage.

Notes

- Store in an airtight container in the refrigerator for 3 to 4 days or in the freezer for up to 1 month.
- Organ meats, like liver, are extremely rich in key nutrients. Beef liver is high in protein, copper, iron, and zinc. It's a good source of vitamin A and various B vitamins. Since liver is very rich and offers up way more nutrients than muscle meat, a little goes a long way. Be careful not to overfeed liver or there is a risk of vitamin A overdose. A general guideline: 1 oz. of liver per day for a medium to large dog, and up to 0.5 oz. per day for small dogs.

See this recipe in action on youtube.com/prouddogmom

Chicken Jerky

Ingredients

- Olive oil, to grease wire rack
- 1 pound chicken breast

Directions

1. Preheat the oven to 250°F.
2. Grease a wire rack with olive oil (or coconut oil) and place on top of a cookie sheet. This will allow the air to circulate as the chicken is dehydrating. Set aside.
3. Trim chicken of all visible fat.
4. Slice the chicken between ⅛" to ¼" thick.
5. Place the chicken slices on a rack and cook for 2 hours.
6. Flip them over after 2 hours and continue to dehydrate in the oven for another 45 minutes, or until fully crisp.

Notes

- Want to change up the flavor? Sprinkle a conservative amount of dog-approved spices onto the chicken strips before putting them in the oven. My two favorite combos are: Ground ginger and ground turmeric with a pinch of ground black pepper.
- Cook time may vary depending on how thick you slice your chicken and your oven.
- Since there are no preservatives added to this jerky, I personally like to keep them in an airtight container in the refrigerator for up to 2 weeks. I doubt you'll have a problem finishing them, though. Along with the dogs, my husband and I like to munch on these treats too!

See this recipe in action on youtube.com/prouddogmom

Wiggly, Jiggly Chicken Gelatin Treats

Ingredients

- ¼ pound chicken breast, all visible fat trimmed
- 1 large carrot, washed, peeled, and chopped
- 3-4 parsley leaves, (or 1 sprig)
- Water, for boiling (will need to reserve ½ cup)
- 1 (.25 oz) packet Knox gelatin powder (plain, unflavored, and unsweetened) OR 1 tablespoon of Great Lakes unflavored gelatin powder

Directions

1. Add chicken breast, chopped carrot, and parsley leaves to a saucepan. Fill with enough water to cover.
2. On medium heat, let cook for about 30 minutes. When finished, the chicken breast will be fully cooked, the carrots will be soft, and the water will be infused with flavor.
3. Leaving your freshly made chicken broth in the saucepan, transfer the cooked chicken and carrots to a blender. Purée until smooth. Set aside.
4. Measure ½ cup of warm chicken broth and transfer to a mixing bowl. Add gelatin powder and whisk until the gelatin is fully dissolved.
5. Stir the puréed chicken and carrot mixture into the gelatin-laden chicken broth until smooth. It should have a gravy-like consistency.
6. Place a silicone mold onto a baking sheet for support and spoon the mixture into each mold, filling to the top.
7. Move to the refrigerator for 1 to 2 hours, or until fully set.

Notes

- While this treat is perfect for dogs of all ages, I originally created this recipe as a joint supplement for my aging Chihuahua. If you're simply looking to create a fun, wiggly, jiggly treat your canine kid will enjoy then Knox plain/unflavored gelatin powder is perfect. However, it's important to note, not all gelatin is created equal. So, if you're looking to reap the most health benefits from these treats then try the Great Lakes unflavored gelatin powder.
- Remove gelatin treats from their mold and transfer to an airtight container. Store in the refrigerator for up to 4 days.
- While these treats may remind you of Jell-O or gummy bears, don't feed your dog store-bought gelatin treats made for people. They include other ingredients that aren't good for dogs.

▶ *See this recipe in action on youtube.com/prouddogmom*

Savory Dog Cake

Ingredients

For the Cake

- ¼ pound lean ground beef
- Half of a large carrot, washed and peeled
- 3–4 broccoli florets
- ¼ cup quick oats
- 1 large egg

For the Icing

- 1 sweet potato
- Half can of salmon, (skinless, boneless, in water, no salt added)

Directions

Make the Cake

1. Preheat the oven to 350°F.
2. Measure meat and put it into a large mixing bowl. Set aside.
3. In a food processor, chop carrot and broccoli. Pulse several times, until you're left with teeny tiny veggie pieces. But, don't overprocess or veggies may become mushy. Add to the mixing bowl.
4. Add remaining cake ingredients into the mixing bowl. Using your hands, mix everything together until thoroughly combined.
5. Press meat mixture into a greased mini-springform pan. Bake for about 50 minutes.

Make the Icing

1. About 15 minutes before your dog cake is finished baking, begin prepping the icing. Using a fork, poke holes into the sweet potato. Microwave for about 7 minutes, or until soft.
2. Let sweet potato cool.
3. Once cooled, scrape the potato into a mixing bowl. Ditch the skin!
4. Drain canned salmon and add half to sweet potato. Using a fork, mash together until thoroughly combined. Set aside until the cake is out of the oven and cooled.

Ice the Cake

1. Once your dog cake is out of the oven and cool enough to handle, use a sharp knife to cut off the top. This will create a flat surface before icing.
2. Either with an icing spatula or your hands, use the sweet potato/salmon mixture to ice your dog cake.

Notes

- Cut the cake into smaller, bite-sized pieces before serving to your dog (to avoid a choking hazard).
- Store cake in an airtight container in the refrigerator for up to 3 days. If you have leftover cake after 3 days, slice and freeze (like you would a meatloaf) for up to 1 month.
- If you don't have lean ground beef, you can swap for lean ground turkey.

See this recipe in action on youtube.com/prouddogmom

Reference Guide

YES/NO "HUMAN FOODS" FOR DOGS

YES

Anchovies
Apples *(avoid the seeds)*
Almond Butter
Asparagus
Bananas
Beef
Bell Peppers
Blueberries
Broccoli
Brussels Sprouts
Cantaloupe
Carrots
Celery
Cheese *(avoid very rich, fatty cheeses, as well as cheeses that contain any herbs*
that are considered toxic to dogs)
Chia Seeds
Chicken
Coconut Oil
Cranberries
Cucumbers
Eggs
Flaxseeds
Ginger
Green Beans
Kale
Liver *(and Other Organ Meats)*
Mango
Peaches
Peanut Butter *(avoid brands that add xylitol)*
Pears
Pineapple *(fresh, not canned)*
100% pure pumpkin *(only pure pumpkin, not pumpkin pie filling)*
Quinoa
Salmon
Sardines
Spinach
Strawberries
Sweet Potato
Turkey
Turmeric
Watermelon *(avoid the seeds and rind)*
Yogurt
Zucchini

NO

Alcohol
Apple seeds
Cacao Powder
Caffeinated Foods & Beverages *(Like Coffee and Tea)*
Chocolate
Cooked Bones
Fat Trimmings
Garlic
Grapes
Lemons
Macadamia Nuts
Nutmeg
Onions *(Including Chives)*
Pits and Seeds from Fruit
Potato Skins *(Raw)*
Raisins
Rhubarb Leaves
Salt
Sugar
Tomato Greenery *(Unripe Tomatoes, Leaves, and Stems)*
Walnuts
Xylitol *(Used in Some Peanut Butter, Gum, and Candy)*
Yeast Dough

In search of homemade dog biscuit recipes, you may occasionally find honey listed as an ingredient. Just like human babies, puppies under one-year-old, or dogs with a compromised immune system, should avoid raw honey. That's because raw honey contains botulism spores.

For a more detailed list, filled with explanations for why each food is safe or unsafe for Fido, check out my cookbook, Proud Dog Chef: Tail Wagging Good Treat Recipes. It's filled with 60 gluten-free and grain-free treat recipes that are bound to make your pup's tail wag.

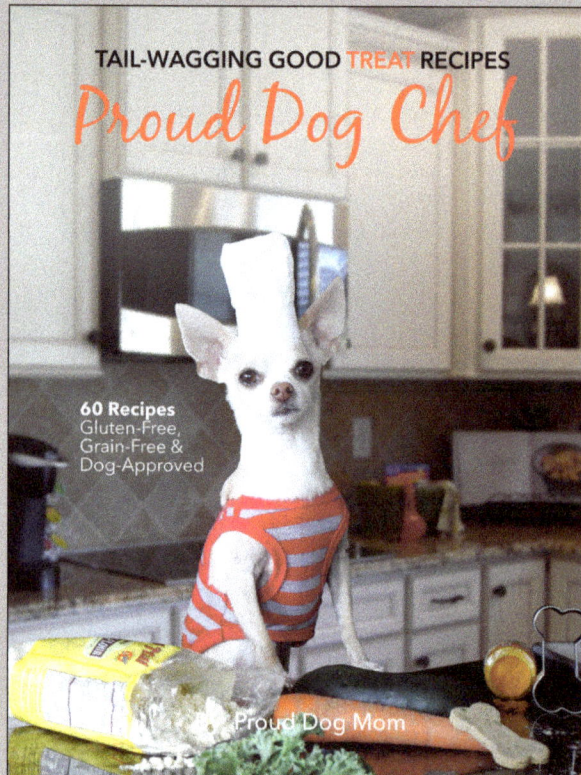

TAIL-WAGGING GOOD TREAT RECIPES
Proud Dog Chef

60 Recipes
Gluten-Free,
Grain-Free &
Dog-Approved

Proud Dog Mom

CHAPTER 10

Puppy Exercise: Mind & Body

Let's keep chatting about ways we can enrich our dogs' lives, promoting health and happiness. Just like with people, regular exercise is essential to canine wellness. It keeps the excess pounds off, promotes a healthy heart and lungs, helps build strong muscles and bones, increases your pup's mood, and even decreases some behavioral issues (*such as destructive chewing, excessive barking,* *etc.*). But, did you know there's such a thing as too much exercise for puppies?

A puppy's bones are still soft and spongy *(they aren't as dense as adult dogs)*, their growth plates haven't closed, and their bodies are continuing to develop. So, over-exercising puppies can negatively impact their musculoskeletal development. This is especially the case for large breed puppies.

HOW MUCH PHYSICAL EXERCISE DOES MY DOG NEED?

Consider Your Dog's Age

In general, short, low-impact, controlled activity sessions each day are best for puppies. While there is no exact science to how much exercise your puppy needs each day, many veterinarians and canine experts recommend the five-minute rule. Basically, it means puppies need five minutes of exercise per month of age, up to twice a day. So, that would mean an exercise session for a three-month-old puppy should last a maximum of 15 minutes.

As your dog matures, you'll work up to longer walks, hikes, and maybe even more challenging activities, like agility. Most adult dogs should get between 30 minutes and two hours of exercise every day.

As adult dogs become senior canines, they'll still need daily movement. But, not as much. Typically, senior dogs need about 30 to 60 minutes of exercise per day, broken into two or more activity sessions.

Consider Your Dog's Breed

Hunting, swimming, herding, and other working dog breeds—like Labrador retrievers, German shepherds, huskies, and border collies—will require more exercise. Toy breeds—such as the Chihuahua and Maltese—don't require quite as much.

If you have a short-nosed breed—like a pug or bulldog—be mindful of exercise amount and intensity. These short-muzzled pups have impeded airflow, putting them at a higher risk of heat exhaustion and oxygen deprivation.

Consult With Your Veterinarian

At the end of the day, every dog's needs are unique. Keep an eye on your pup's limits, watch for signs of tiredness, and never push them. If you have any questions or concerns regarding your dog's activity level, consult with your vet.

MENTAL STIMULATION

Along with moving their body, there's another type of exercise our pups need. It's called mental stimulation and, just like it sounds, it literally means you're exercising your dog's mind. Like people, dogs get bored. And do you know what happens when a dog gets bored? Yup! They find creative ways to amuse themselves. *(In ways we usually don't like. Think: excessive barking, destructive chewing, digging holes, etc.)*

By providing mental stimulation for your dog, you're helping to:

- Bust doggy boredom
- Put an end to unwanted behaviors that are triggered by boredom
- Lower stress levels and improve mood
- Burn off energy/tire out your dog
- Keep your dog's mind sharp

There are a variety of ways you can fire up your dog's mind.

Enrichment Walks

Not all dog walks are created equal. Sometimes, you and your pup will head out for a quick potty break. Other times, you may leash up your furry friend to work on obedience training. Then, there are leisure walks where you let your dog leave the heel position to explore his surroundings, sniff around, check the pee-mail, and just be a dog. These are perhaps the most satisfying walks for your pooch because a dog's nose is the window to his world. Giving Fido time to sniff the grass, nearby bushes, and poles is mentally enriching.

Work on New Tricks

If your dog already knows the basic commands, why not work on cool trick training? Spending just 15 minutes every day to work on commands and tricks is a great way to fire up your pup's mind and get him to focus on something meaningful … all while strengthening your communication and bond!

Agility Training

Have you ever watched those athletic dogs on television gracefully yet speedily going through obstacle courses where they weave in between poles, run through tunnels, jump over objects, and walk over seesaws? Well, that's called dog agility … and wow is it fun! If your pup has a lot of energy, enjoys being active, and thrives when learning new tricks then he may love this sport. Dogs usually start competing in agility trials between one to two years old, and can get started with training a little before that. While it's best to hold off on jumps until your puppy's body is a bit more mature *(to avoid injury)*, this is a wonderful way to both physically and mentally enrich your dog. If you're interested, look to see if there is an agility training group near you. Or, if you just want to have some fun with it at home, you can always purchase or DIY a practice course of your own.

Socialize

Whenever your dog meets a new person or pet, their senses heighten. They're seeing new faces, hearing new sounds, and smelling new butts. You know how it goes—*Getting to know you, getting to know all about you. Getting to like you, getting to hope you like me!* Socialization is beneficial for so many reasons, and mental stimulation makes the list.

Interactive Toys and Puzzles

Game night, anyone? In my house, if you open up the game closet, you'll find a stack of my favorite board games on the left and a stack of my dogs' favorite puzzles on the right. That's right, there are puzzles and interactive toys that are made specifically for dogs.

There are a variety of puzzles on the market. While they each require slightly different problem-solving skills and offer various challenge levels, they all have one thing in common: You hide treats somewhere in the puzzle and your dog has to figure out how to get them out. The top puzzle brands to check out are Outward Hound, Trixie, Planet Dog, and KONG.

MAKE-YOUR-OWN KONG STUFFING RECIPE (IN 3 SIMPLE STEPS)

The classic KONG is a durable rubber toy with a hollow center that you stuff with Fido-friendly foods and treats. It's a cross between a food bowl and a boredom-buster enrichment puzzle that provides dogs with a healthy outlet to chew and lick. Depending on your dog's size, the KONG comes in XS all the way to XXL! Here is KONG's sizing chart:

- XS—Up to 5 lbs
- S—Up to 20 lbs
- M—15-35 lbs
- L—30-65 lbs
- XL—60-90 lbs
- XXL—85+ lbs

While I generally don't like giving my dogs rubber toys, this popular and versatile plaything is super thick and durable. Plus, they offer various rubber intensities based on your dog's chewing style. The KONG comes in:

- Puppy—Baby blue or baby pink
- Classic—Red
- Extreme—Black
- Senior—Purple

How to Stuff Your KONG Toy

Beginners—If your dog has never played with a classic KONG toy before, I recommend starting with something super easy. Fill the center of your KONG with a few small, loose treats. Use your dog's favorite biscuit recipe or another treat that makes him go wild. Then, give it to your pooch to roll around and work out the tasty reward. Chances are, the loose treats will fall out pretty quickly. But, it will teach your dog that something yummy goes inside.

Intermediate—Next, bump it up a notch with a more robust mixture. When crafting your KONG stuffing recipe, pick one ingredient from each of the following categories, and then mix the ingredients together. Tightly pack them into the center of your classic KONG and let your pooch work it out!

Choose a Base

1. 100% pure pumpkin purée
2. Sweet potato
3. Applesauce
4. Plain Greek yogurt
5. Cottage cheese
6. Cooked oatmeal
7. Cooked quinoa
8. Mashed banana

Choose a Yummy Booster

1. Boiled and shredded chicken
2. Boiled and puréed steak (*a cheap cut is great as long as it's very lean*)
3. Lean ground beef, cooked
4. Lean ground turkey, cooked
5. Mashed canned salmon (*plain, in water, drained*)
6. Sardines (*plain, in water, drained*)
7. Peanut butter
8. Almond butter

Choose a Healthy Add-In

1. Shredded carrots
2. Shredded zucchini

3. Finely chopped broccoli
4. Finely shredded Brussels sprouts
5. Finely chopped kale
6. Chopped spinach
7. Diced red bell pepper
8. Smashed blueberries
9. Finely diced strawberries

Some Great Combinations

- Applesauce + chicken + carrots
- Pumpkin purée + steak or ground beef + broccoli
- Sweet potato + salmon + spinach
- Cottage cheese + one mashed sardine + red bell pepper
- Applesauce + ground turkey + finely chopped spinach
- Plain Greek yogurt + ground turkey + finely chopped kale
- Mashed banana + peanut butter + strawberries

Advanced — Follow the same recipe building formula as outlined above, but pop the KONG in the freezer for about four hours (*or overnight*) before giving it to your pooch. It will take your dog a lot longer to lick and work out the yummy reward.

See these DIY tutorials in action on youtube.com/prouddogmom

DIY DOG PUZZLES TO MAKE RIGHT NOW

Along with all the interactive toys and puzzles you find in the store, you can also make your own at home using common household items!

Snuffle Mat

A snuffle mat is a popular nose work, brain game. It consists of fleece fabric strips tied onto a sturdy backing. You hide dog treats inside the fleece—behind the many folds and deep inside where the fleece meets the backing—for your dog to sniff out, find, and then eat.

The idea behind this simple yet genius game is to mimic the foraging and hunting activities our dogs' wild ancestors engaged in regularly. From developing puppies to aging seniors, this enrichment toy is perfect for all dogs.

While you can buy a snuffle mat from an online retailer or pet store, you can easily make one yourself. It's inexpensive, fun to put together, and super rewarding when you watch your dog enjoying your creation.

Supplies

- Rubber Sink Mat—To use as your base
- Fleece—I like to use two colors to create variation. The exact amount will depend on the size of your mat and the width of the strips you cut. I used some cheap fleece blankets.
- Scissors—To cut the fleece into strips
- Mini screwdriver, skewer stick, or capped pen (optional)—To help you easily push the fabric through the base

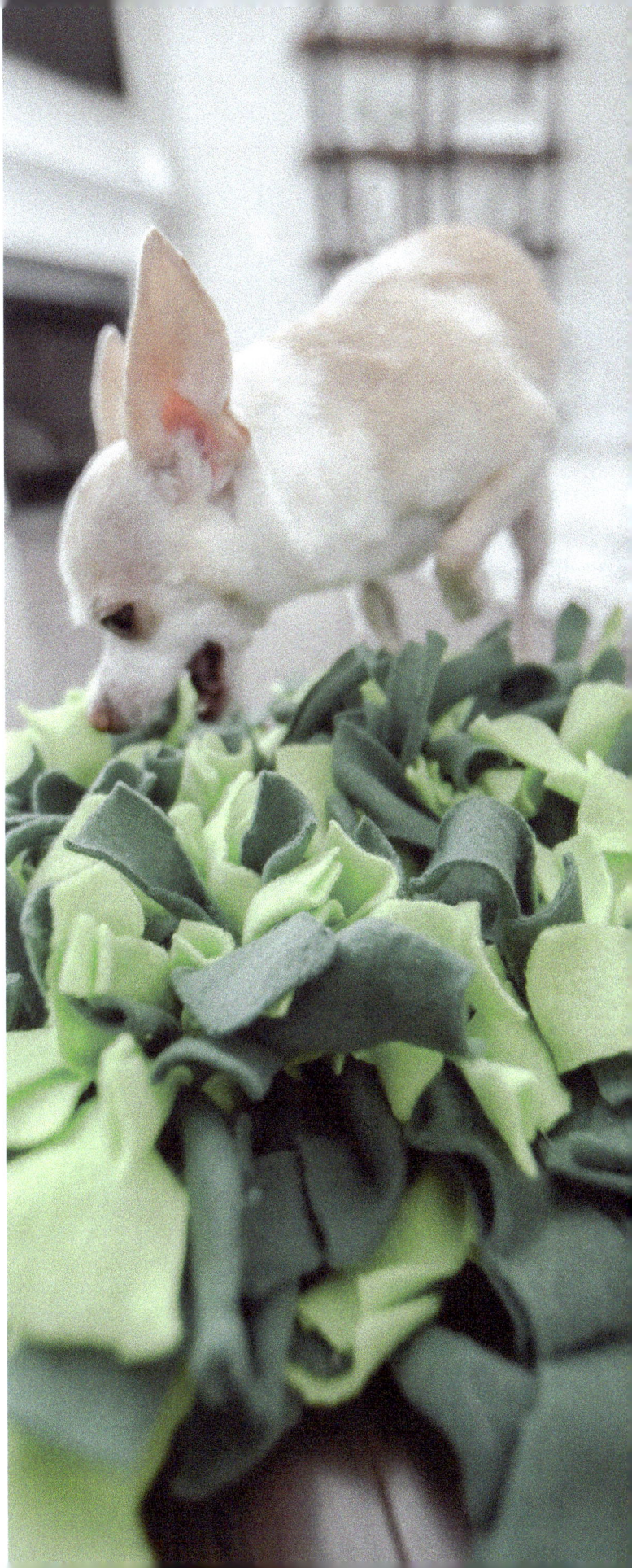

Directions

1. Cut the fleece into strips. Aim to get your strips 1" wide by 6 to 8" long. This doesn't have to be perfect. Some can be a little longer or shorter than others. For my 12.5" x 11" sink mat, I needed 260 strips. *(So, 130 strips of each color if you are following my same pattern.)*

2. Weave the fleece strips through the mat, starting with a hole in the upper corner. Take one end of a fleece strip and push it through the hole closest to the mat's edge. Then, push the opposite end through the very next hole. Flip the mat over and tie a knot.

3. Moving in the same direction, repeat Step #2 until the entire mat is covered with fleece.

Up until this point, you'll want to stick to one color.

4. With your second fleece color, repeat Step #2 and Step #3 in the opposite direction. Since there will be a lot of fleece on the mat by this time, you may want to use a mini screwdriver, skewer stick, or capped pen to help you easily push the fabric through.

If your dog has never played with a snuffle mat before, place his favorite treats on top of the fleece strips, give it to your dog, and let him munch away. Then, on the next round, increase the challenge by burying the treats a little deeper into the strips. I promise your dog will get the hang of it in no time!

Muffin Tin Puzzle

For this puzzle, grab a muffin tin, some treats, and up to 12 balls. Start by simply dropping a treat into each cup in the muffin tin. Then, cover it with a ball. If you don't have 12 tennis or rubber balls, you can also use a classic KONG or even a small plush toy. Get creative!

When starting out, I suggest covering half the spaces. That way, your dog easily spots some yummy treats and feels more eager to scoot the balls over, searching for hidden snacks. Each time you play, add more balls until each cup is covered, or change up the pattern!

Busy Box

Also called an enrichment box, foraging box, or destruction box, a busy box is a super simple DIY interactive puzzle that dogs love. You start with a basic cardboard box. Using a sharp knife, poke one or two thin holes on each side of the cardboard box. *This step is optional, but it helps your dog get a better whiff of what's inside.* Then, fill it up with your dog's favorite toys, balls, and random stuff lying around your home. Items you can stuff treats inside are gold! You can also sprinkle in a few loose treats to enhance the whole experience. Lightly close the box and give it to your dog to open and forage through.

Towel Roll-Up

In the busy box, I like to add a treat-filled towel. Basically, I grab a clean washcloth or dish towel, drop several lines of treats, and roll up the towel.

Well, this alone is a great game for your pup. Once you roll your dog's favorite treats inside an old (*yet clean*) towel or blanket, place it on the ground and let him unravel it to free the treats and eat the yummy snacks!

> ▶ See these DIY tutorials in action on youtube.com/prouddogmom

CHAPTER 11

Cleaning with Canines

CHORE LIST

When I first welcomed Diego and Gigi into my family, I lived in a two-bedroom apartment in west Texas. After a few years, I packed up our things and moved back east, closer to my family near Charlotte, North Carolina. As soon as I had enough money saved up, I bought my furbabies a house. Every day, we would drive by the property to watch the builders install floors, walls, the roof, cabinets, and then the finishing touches. As I sat there in awe, I remember looking down at my dogs and saying, *"Look what I did! I bought you a house!"* It was one of the proudest moments of my life.

I love watching my dogs thoroughly enjoy our home, as they run up and down the carpet-lined stairs, spread their many toys across the floor, snooze on the off-white couches, and get cozy in the bed for a good night's sleep. Yes, my canine kids are allowed on the furniture. I wouldn't have it any other way.

As much as I adore my pups, I'm also pretty obsessed with keeping a clean house. Here's the good news: It is possible to keep your home free of muddy paw prints, nose smudges, and shedding pet hair.

I like to break up my cleaning schedule by Daily, Weekly, Monthly tasks. This step-by-step guide is filled with a simple cleaning schedule, pet-safe cleaning products, and tools to make your space sparkle!

Daily
Vacuum the Living Room and High-Traffic Areas in Your Home. Along with a regular vacuum, I recommend investing in a robot vacuum! I've had mine for several years and it's made daily chores a breeze. Every day, I turn it on and it cleans my hardwood,

area rugs, and carpets. When it's done, it self-docs and recharges. All I have to do is dump out the dog hair, dander, grass, and any dust it collected during its ride around my house.

Pick up All Dog Toys Lying Around the Floor. I keep my pup's plush, rubber, and rope toys organized in a special basket. Mine is metal and has a cute dog-related saying on it. So, I display it in its own little doggy corner in my master bedroom. There are also cute wicker baskets in the shape of a bone. Now, *those* are precious!

Wash Your Dog's Food and Water Bowls. If you neglect your puppy's water bowl, it will develop a thick, gooey, slimy substance called biofilm. While biofilm does contain some good bacteria, it also contains bad bacteria that can make your dog sick. Listeria and E. coli both call biofilm home. Bad biofilms have been linked to urinary tract infections (UTIs), bladder infections, ear infections, and more. To avoid this buildup from happening, you just have to wash your dog's bowl! Throughout the day, every time you refill your dog's bowls, wipe them down with a paper towel to physically break up any biofilm that's forming. Then, at the end of the day, wash the bowls in hot water by hand. You can also put them in the dishwasher once a week for a deeper clean.

Clean Doggy Doo Doo From the Backyard. If you have a backyard, don't start collecting doggy poop piles. *That's just gross!* Instead, every day, grab the waste bags and go pick it up. Since my community's trash pickup is once a week, I keep a mini trash can in the backyard specifically for doo doo-filled waste bags.

Here's an Extra Tip: Keep paw wipes near your door and give your puppy's paws a quick clean after walks. Have you ever thought about the bacteria buildup on your puppy's paws? If not, let's take a second to do that. Since most dogs don't wear shoes, they're constantly outside walking through grass, dirt, urine, and feces. Then, they come inside, prance around your area rugs, drag their paws along the carpets, and jump on your furniture. That's why I like to keep a pack of paw wipes near the door. I give their tootsies a quick wash when they get inside and it makes me feel a whole lot cleaner!

Weekly

Scan Your Floors With a Black Light. No one likes a smelly house. No one. To check for surprise puppy pee-pee accidents that could spark unwanted odors, wait until the evening when it's dark, turn off all interior lights, grab a blacklight, and scan your entire house. Holding the blacklight about one to two inches away from the carpet, furniture, or mattress, slowly check every room, corner, and crevice. Keep an eye out for light yellow fluorescent glowing spots. Even well-trained dogs can occasionally let out a little squirt. That's why it's called an *accident*. If you find any urine spots, clean them up with an enzyme-based cleaning solution that will neutralize the odors and remove the stain. It's important to find and treat urine spots so your dog doesn't keep smelling and marking over and over. More on how to clean urine drenched carpet on page 148.

Mop/Wash Floors With a Natural Cleaning Product. Every time you wash your floor with toxic chemicals and Fido walks across it, he's exposed to the residues left behind. Even once the cleaner dries, it can absorb through his paw pads and into his bloodstream. Plus, each time your pup eats something off the floor, or licks the floor, he's ingesting residual cleaners. So, when it comes to mopping your floor, either use a natural store-bought product or make your own solution.

- *Tile, Stone, and Vinyl Flooring:* In a bucket, mix 1 gallon of warm tap water with 1 cup of distilled white vinegar. Mop the floor as usual. There's no need to rinse the floor after!

- *Hardwoods:* Add 1 quart of distilled water and 1/4 cup of distilled white vinegar to a spray bottle. Spray on the floor and then use a microfiber pad mop to spread and dry. *Only use this on sealed hardwoods and always follow any specific cleaning instructions given by your floor's manufacturer.*

Remove Dog Hair From Couches. I usually do this by vacuuming the couches with a hand-held vacuum and then using the rubber glove hack to pick up any remaining hairs. Just put a rubber glove on one hand, slightly dampen the glove, and then run your hand across the couch cushions. You'll be amazed at how much hair it collects.

Extra Tip: To keep couches clean, use a waterproof couch protector. For years, I just decorated my couches in blankets. But, if I'm being honest, they always looked horrible. I remember scrambling before guests arrived because I didn't want them to see the couch rags. Now, I use neutral color and clean-looking protectors designed for families with pets.

Clean Glass Surfaces to Remove Doggy Nose Artwork. If you're looking for a DIY all-natural cleaner, try mixing 1 part distilled white vinegar to 10 parts warm water in a spray bottle.

Dust Tables and Surfaces With a Microfiber Cloth. Neither you nor your dog should breathe in the dust!

Clean Toilet Bowls. We've all seen images of dogs dipping their heads into a toilet and taking a little lick of the water. The biggest danger to Fido is

the chemicals used to clean the bowl. Commercial cleaning agents contain toxins that can be harmful to your pooch. This includes chemical-laden cleaning wands, disinfectant tablets that turn the water blue, and deodorizers that cling onto the side of the bowl. For this reason, I highly suggest keeping lids closed.

With that said, you can also try swapping chemicals for distilled white vinegar! For weekly cleaning, just pour 1/2 cup of distilled white vinegar into the water, swishy it around, let it sit for about 30 minutes, swish again, and flush. Viola! If you have hard water then you may want to bump it up to 1 full cup of vinegar and let it sit for an hour. If you need even more muscle for your cleaner, you can pour 1/2 cup of baking soda into the toilet, followed by 1 cup of vinegar. It will create a volcano effect. Let it sit for 10 minutes, swish it around, and then flush.

Wash Bedding Sheets. Wash your sheets at least weekly to rid your bed of excess hairs from shedding and dander.

Monthly

Wash Your Dog's Toys. Dog toys are slobbered on and dragged across the floor *(for way more than five seconds)*. With everything those toys are exposed to, they're filled with bacteria. That's why they need to be cleaned from time-to-time.

- *Plush Toys:* Just toss the dirty toys in your washing machine! Skip the laundry detergent and sprinkle the toys with a little baking soda and a few capfuls of white vinegar. Once the cycle is done, pop those babies into the dryer. Make sure your dryer is set to low or air-only. You can also let the toys air dry. In case you're wondering: Yes, the squeakers still work afterward!

- *Hard Toys:* Most hard rubber and rope toys can be cleaned in the dishwasher. Load your dog's hard toys on the top rack and let them go for a spin. Just make sure to skip the dish detergent and use distilled white vinegar instead. The hot water and pressure alone should kill the germs, but the vinegar will give it a little extra power.

Wash Dog Bedding and Apparel. Most are machine washable but double-check labels before popping them in for a spin.

Wash Dog Collars. Simply submerge your dog's collar in a tub of hot water with a few drops of natural pet shampoo. Soak for about 30 minutes, rinse with water, and then hang to dry.

Touch Up Wall Scuffs. Has your puppy's wagging tail left a few scuff marks on the wall? I don't like letting house projects build up. So, to avoid a large collection of wall scuffs, I bust out the touch-up paint once a month and clean up the walls.

Take Stock of Pet Supplies. Order any waste bags, natural cleaning supplies, grooming tools, food, medications, or anything else your dog needs. Nothing is more frustrating than going to fetch something you need only to find out there's none left!

NATURAL CLEANING INGREDIENTS TO KEEP HANDY

Distilled White Vinegar

This is the *King Of The Road* of non-toxic, pet safe cleansers. Found in most household pantries, it's cheap, edible, cleans, and deodorizes. The reason vinegar is so potent is because of its acetic acid content. With a pH around 3, it has the power to cut through grease, dirt, mineral deposits/stains from hard water, and can kill various forms of bacteria, viruses, fungi, and molds.

White vinegar can be used straight out of the bottle, diluted, or in combination with an assortment of natural pet-friendly ingredients. *Warning: Vinegar is too harsh for some surfaces and should not be used on granite or marble, as it can cause pitting.*

Baking Soda

Baking soda is another natural powerful cleaning staple you likely have in the pantry. The chemical name for baking soda is *sodium* bicarbonate and, as its chemical name implies, it's a *salt*. With a pH of 9, it's considered alkaline *(opposite of an acid).*

Baking soda absorbs odors, disinfects, kills molds, dissolves dirt, grease, and grime. Pop open a box to keep your refrigerator smelling fresh. Sprinkle it straight from the box and use it as you'd use any scouring powder. Or mix it with water to form a paste and use it as a soft scrub.

Lemons and Lemon Juice

The almighty lemon not only makes things smell clean, but it also touts antibacterial and antifungal properties. With a pH of 2, this acid can blast through dirt, grease, and grime.

3% Hydrogen Peroxide

A staple in many bathroom cabinets, hydrogen peroxide is a disinfectant. It's effective against various microorganisms, such as bacteria, yeast, fungi, some viruses, and molds. Hydrogen peroxide can be used right from the bottle—no need to mix it with anything. Does it get any easier than that? Just pop a spray top on to the brown bottle, grab a rag and you're ready to clean.

Use it in the bathroom in sinks and toilets, in the kitchen on countertops and appliances, as a glass and mirror cleaner, to disinfect garbage cans, and all around the house. Give it a chance to work—spray it on, wait a few minutes, and then wipe.

IMPORTANT NOTE: *Keep Hydrogen Peroxide in its dark bottle or it will break down and become water. If the peroxide isn't bubbling when you use it, it's no longer active. Toss it and replace the bottle.*

NEVER *mix hydrogen peroxide and vinegar in the same bottle. The combination forms peracetic acid, which is a caustic acid that can be harmful to the skin, eyes, and respiratory system.*

HOW TO PROPERLY CLEAN PET URINE OUT OF CARPETS

Accidents happen. The reality is, at some point, all dog parents will deal with a little pee on the floor. As you potty train your puppy, proper clean up is essential.

When a dog pees on the carpet, urine soaks down through the bristles and spreads into the padding. So, the spot's size may be larger than what you see. If you're not properly cleaning up urine, your dog will still smell the lingering odor and may continue to have accidents in that spot. Another issue: A strong urine odor will begin to fill the room. No one wants to take a big whiff of urine!

Soak It up Completely

Ideally, you want to clean up pet urine when it's freshly served and still wet. Start by placing several layers of paper towels—or another absorbent cloth/towel—over the soiled area. Apply pressure to the wet area, absorbing as much liquid as you can. Depending on how much urine is in the carpet, you may need to repeat this step several times with fresh towels.

Dilute It

Pour plain, cool water over the soiled area to help dilute the urine mess. Then, use more paper towels—or a clean absorbent cloth/towel—to pull out the excess moisture. Repeat until you don't see any more yellow liquid left on the towels.

Use an Enzyme-Based Cleaner

To blast away any lingering smell, use an enzymatic cleaner. Enzymes are proteins that break up urine molecules and dissolve odors. There are plenty of store-bought options to choose from, like Nature's Miracle and Simple Solution. Whichever brand you pick, just make sure it's an enzyme-based cleaner that's formulated for pet messes, eliminating odors, and destroying stains. Generously spray the store-bought cleaner on and around the soiled area and let sit for about 10 to 15 minutes, or as instructed on the back of the bottle. Blot the excess moisture with paper towels, or another clean absorbent cloth/ towel. Vacuum the area once dry. If necessary, repeat this step.

Prefer to make your own cleaning solution? There are various DIY recipes—some use vinegar, while others use hydrogen peroxide. I personally find hydrogen peroxide solutions work best to blast away foul odors.

- Liberally apply baking soda over the soiled area.
- In a bottle, mix 1 teaspoon of Dawn dishwashing liquid with 1/2 cup of 3% hydrogen peroxide.
- Pour the mixture over the stain and baking soda, and scrub the area with a cloth or brush.
- Let the mixture sit for about 10 to 15 minutes.
- Blot the excess moisture with a paper towel. Vacuum thoroughly once the area is dry.
- Repeat for stubborn soils.

IMPORTANT NOTE: *Test this solution on a small section first to ensure the hydrogen peroxide doesn't discolor your carpet.*

CLEANING OLDER CARPET STAINS

It's best to clean pet messes right away. But, sometimes, pee squirts go unnoticed and you don't find them until later *(that's why I recommend weekly blacklight checks)*. If you discover a dried urine mess on your carpet, follow the same steps as above. But, keep in mind, when it comes to older messes, you may have to repeat the process several times before the stain and lingering odor is completely dissolved.

For extra help, consider renting or investing in a carpet shampooer. When my dogs went through the puppy phase, Bissell became my best friend. From large, corded shampooers to handheld, cordless devices, I quickly created an arsenal of carpet cleaning products. Plus, there are carpet shampoos formulated specifically to tackle pet messes. You can also enlist a professional carpet cleaning service for help.

In certain cases, you may need to replace portions of the padding and carpet.

What Not to Do

Do not use ammonia-based products to clean pet messes. Since dog urine contains ammonia, these products can actually mimic the smell and make the area even more attractive to your puppy. This ultimately encourages future accidents *(not what we're going for)*.

Additionally, don't ever combine bleach with ammonia. It's extremely dangerous and fumes can be deadly.

Avoid using steam cleaners to clean urine odors from carpet or upholstery, as the heat will permanently set the stain and the odor.

CHAPTER 12

Traveling With Dogs

When they say to only pack the essentials, that means your dog! If you're a travel-lover and dream of having your dog tag-along for great adventures then I've got some great news: Today, there are plenty of pet-friendly cities, activities, events, restaurants, and hotels. So, a fun-filled getaway with your pooch is totally doable!

JUST CAN'T WAIT TO GET ON THE ROAD AGAIN

Planning a road trip with your canine companion? When my furkids were young, they were constantly in the car. Back when I lived in west Texas, we loved to pack up and explore the beautiful southwest. Some weekends, we would just drive a few hours away to neighboring New Mexico. *(If you're looking for somewhere awe-worthy then you've gotta check out White Sands!)* Other times, we would travel a full day to different Texas cities, like Austin. But, back then, nothing beat our cross-country trips to Charlotte, North Carolina to visit family. We would spend an intense two days in the car, checking off states every few hours. Now that we live in the Charlotte area, we love taking beach trips to Charleston, South Carolina and weekend visits to Florida. So, I think it's fair to say my dogs are expert car riders!

Pimp Your Ride
Before you get behind the wheel with your canine co-pilot by your side, take some time to pimp out your ride. No, I'm not talking about installing fancy sub-woofers *(haha "woofers")*. I'm referring to safety gear.

While many pet parents don't restrain their dogs in the car, it's something you should definitely consider. In fact, depending on where you live, your state may require it.

Dogs roaming free without some sort of safety restraint can get really hurt in an accident. To keep this simple and to the point, let's talk about a frontal car crash. Let's also say your car is traveling at a speed of 40 mph. It's important to realize that it's not only your car that's going 40 mph, but, everyone in the car, including your furbaby, is also moving at that speed. So, when a car crashes and suddenly stops, the passengers are still in motion going 40 mph until something stops them. In the case of human passengers, we assume they're wearing a seat belt. But what about your dog? If he isn't restrained, he's going to continue moving like a missile until he hits something *(like the seat in front of him, the dashboard, windshield, or another person in the car)*. Not only does this force pose great harm to your pooch, but he can also harm another passenger.

Car Seats—Just like toddlers have to ride in a car seat, your pooch can benefit from one too. There are various booster seats on the market for small to medium size dogs. Simply strap a properly fitted harness onto your dog, clip him into the booster seat, and take off. Some car seats are designed to fit on top of a car's center console, others fasten nicely on a passenger's seat *(preferably in the back)*. Along with keeping your pup safe, they allow your dog to sit up high and see out the window as they ride.

Car Harness With Seat Belt Attachment—If you do a quick search online, you'll also find dog harnesses that attach to a car's seat belt. These are another great restraining option. *NOTE: Only use these restraining devices with an approved harness and **never** hook a restraint to a collar. If the dog is tethered to a collar and the car is in an accident, there is always a risk your dog will get thrown around and hang himself.*

Crate—If you have an SUV and your dog rides in a cargo area, you can use a dog crate that's appropriate for travel. If your dog is in a crate, make sure it's secured to something so it won't go flying in case of an accident.

Getting Familiar With the Car

When your dog is still a young puppy, this is the perfect time to get your furkid familiar with the car. Start by sitting with your pup in a stationary car. Introduce him to his car seat or preferred safety restraint. Offer treats and lots of praise! Once your pup seems calm and comfortable, go for a quick ride around the block. Start with small trips and work your way up to longer car rides.

If your puppy shows any signs of motion sickness, avoid feeding him before a ride and crack open the windows while moving. Lowering the windows by a couple of inches while driving can help balance out the air pressure, possibly reducing your dog's nausea. Plus, since hot and stuffy temperatures can add fuel to the *car sickness* fire, a little air can go a long way. If all else fails, talk to your veterinarian about anti-nausea medicine.

What to Pack

- Food and water
- A small cooler to keep food, water, and any medications cool
- Portable food and water bowls
- Treats
- Any medications your pup may need
- Leash *(pack a second one as backup)*
- Spare collar or harness
- Waste bags
- Paper towels
- Blankets
- Toys
- Pet first aid kit
- Flea comb and tick remover *(just in case this isn't in your pet first aid kit!)*
- Medical records showing proof of vaccines
- Proper ID
- A current photo of your dog *(in case your pup is to ever bolt at a rest stop and get lost)*

HOW TO INTRODUCE YOUR DOG TO A CARRIER

Place the Carrier in a Room Where Your Dog Hangs Out

The first step is to introduce your puppy to the pet carrier in a non-intimidating way. So, place the carrier on the floor of your living room, bedroom, or another room where your dog spends a lot of time. With the carrier's door open, let your pup explore without hovering over him. Let the carrier sit open on the floor for a few days.

Make the Carrier a Fun Place

Once your dog is used to seeing the carrier, start putting his stuff in it — a thin blanket, maybe his favorite toy, and even some treats. This will entice your dog to walk inside and ultimately realize the carrier isn't a *scary* thing.

Try Closing the Door

Once your pooch is going into the carrier on his own, try closing the door for a few seconds and then open it back up before he has time to react.

Reward with a yummy treat and plenty of praise. Repeat this step several times over the next day or two, gradually extending the length of time the door is closed.

Walk Around With Your Pup in the Carrier

Once your dog is comfortable with the carrier door being closed, pick up the bag and walk around with him inside. I recommend trying this in your home, backyard, or neighborhood first. This will help get him used to the motions.

Go Out in Public

If you're planning to use the carrier in airports and other public places then I recommend popping your pooch in his carrier and heading down to the mall or another public place close to your home. This will help get your dog used to being in the carrier while surrounded by other people.

LESSONS LEARNED FROM FLYING WITH MY DOG

Typically, when I go jet-setting, my two furkids head off to their grandparents' house and enjoy a week of extra treats and pampering. But, there are times when they come along for the ride. If you're considering flying with your pup, you'll have a couple of choices: Dogs can either fly in the cabin with you or in the cargo area. Flying cargo is incredibly stressful and dangerous for dogs. I wouldn't recommend it. Instead, you want them right by your side in the main cabin.

Research Flights ASAP

When looking into flights for you and your dog, start your search as early as possible. Check out every airline to see which offers a direct flight, or a flight with the fewest layovers.

Reserve a Spot on the Plane for Your Pooch

Before booking your tickets, call the airline and let them know you'll be flying with your dog. You'll need to reserve a spot for your canine companion ASAP, as there are only a handful of in-cabin spots available per flight. The first time I flew with Diego, the airline only allowed two dogs in the main cabin. You don't want to book your tickets, arrive at the airport with your dog, and then find out there's no room for your pup!

It's also a good idea to give the airline a call back 24 to 48 hours before your flight to reconfirm your pup's spot is reserved.

Expect to Pay Extra

If your pup isn't considered an emotional support or service dog then you can expect to pay an extra fee.

Ask the airline's customer service representatives about exact pricing.

Get a Health Certificate From Your Vet

Before you say, "Bon Voyage," schedule a visit with your vet for a full health check. While you're there, ask for an official health certificate (*AKA a document that states your dog is in good health and shows his vaccines are up to date*) and make sure it's signed by the vet. Check with your carrier, as each airline has specific rules to follow before your pup's paws are permitted to touch down on the tarmac.

You Must Check-in at the Ticket Counter

Whenever I fly, I like to check-in 24-hours in advance on my phone. At that time, I get my mobile boarding passes and upload them to Apple's Wallet app. I do this to avoid the long check-in line at the airport and cut straight to the security line. But, when you're traveling with a dog, you must check-in at the ticket counter.

Your Dog's Carrier Counts as One of Your Carry-On Bags

Every time I fly, I bring one larger bag that gets stored in the overhead bin above my seat and my purse, which stays on the floor under the seat in front of me. When you travel with a dog in the main cabin, though, their pet carrier replaces one of your carry-on items.

The pet carrier must be placed under the seat in front of you (*never in the overhead bin*). That means, your other carry-on item (*whether it's a purse or larger bag*) must be stored in the overhead bin.

Double-Check Carrier Dimensions

Speaking of pet carriers, it's important to note different airlines and planes have different under-seat dimensions. So, as you're planning for your upcoming trip, double-check the pet carrier size requirements. You can either find this information on the airline's website or you can give them a call and speak with a customer service representative. Regardless, you don't want to sit down and find out your pet carrier doesn't fit under the seat in front of you.

The Cabin Floor Can Get Really Hot or Really Cold During the Flight

The first time I flew with Diego, I was told the cabin floor can get really cold. So, to keep him warm during the flight, I dressed him in a rather thick sweater. Well, the floor blowers weren't turned on during my flight, so Diego got very hot. My advice: Bring a thin blanket in case the floor is cold, but bend down and stick your hand into the pet carrier every 20 to 30 minutes to ensure it's a comfortable temperature.

Tell Your Neighbor About Your Dog

As a common courtesy, I always let my neighboring passengers know when I'm traveling with my dogs. I do this to make sure they don't have any pet allergies. While most people have no issues—and are excited to see a little furball by their feet—it's still nice to inform them a dog is nearby.

Your Pooch May Not Get a Chance to Go to the Bathroom

Since so many people travel with their dogs today, many airports have pet relief stations. That said, I still like to bring pee pads with me just in case. *While we're on the topic, keep pre-flight food and water to a minimum!*

12 PET-FRIENDLY HOTEL ETIQUETTE TIPS

If you're planning to stay in a pet-friendly hotel with your dogs, there are a few etiquette rules I encourage you to follow.

Make Reservations for Your Dog

When booking your stay, verify the hotel is pet-friendly and let the front desk know you'll be traveling with a dog. Ask if there are any extra pet charges or deposits. Plus, find out if they're refundable or non-refundable. You don't want any surprises at check-in.

Never Sneak Your Dog Into the Hotel

With so many pet-friendly hotel chains to choose from, there's no reason to ever sneak your pooch into the room. Truly, you may not get caught. But why risk getting thrown out?

Don't Use the Ice Bucket as a Water Bowl

When you travel with your dog, always bring along food and water bowls. If you accidentally forget them, ask the front desk staff if they can supply some. Whatever you do, don't feed your dog out of the hotel ice bucket or trays. First of all, it's not sanitary for your dog and you don't know what chemical solutions those things have been cleaned with *(or if they've been cleaned at all)*. Secondly, it's not nice to whoever stays in the room after you.

Don't Leave Your Pooch in the Room Alone

There are a few reasons why you shouldn't leave your dog unattended in a hotel room:

- It's against pet policy in most hotels.
- Your pooch has no clue where he is and will likely be frightened if you leave him alone. This is a recipe for disaster. A nervous dog is likely to act out when you're gone. He may chew furniture or claw at the carpet and door in an attempt to escape and find you.
- He'll probably bark uncontrollably, which could result in someone calling in a complaint.

If you need to leave your dog, plan ahead and find a local doggie sitter or daycare. This way, you'll know your pooch is cared for and safe.

Keep Barking to a Minimum

Of course a woof here and a woof there is okay, but don't let your dog bark non-stop. As he gets more comfortable in his new surroundings, he may get territorial and bark as he hears doors opening/closing or people walking down the hall. Hotels say they allow well-behaved dogs, so, if you can't quiet your pooch then he may not be ready for a hotel stay.

Prepare for Accidents

When your canine kid stays in a pet-friendly hotel, he's exposed to various smells from the countless dogs who stayed there before. This could stimulate even the most well-trained dog to perhaps leave a little squirt—or even a little puddle! If your dog is a marker, excited pees, or you just aren't sure what he'll do, you may want to bring a doggy diaper or belly band with you…just in case.

Pack Some Pet Enzyme Odor Cleaner

In case your pooch does have an accident *(or an on purpose)*, it's a good idea to have a little bottle of carpet cleaner that blasts odors and stains.

Don't Let Your Dog Roam Off-Leash

Always keep your dog leashed when walking through the hotel and on the grounds.

- Your dog is in unfamiliar surroundings and may have the urge to wander off and explore. Dogs can easily get lost or even hit by a car in the parking lot if they aren't on their leash.
- There may be other dogs at the hotel and you have no clue if they're friendly. It's much easier to control and protect a dog on a leash, should the need arise.
- It's common courtesy. Other guests may feel uncomfortable and even frightened by an unleashed dog.

Pick Up Your Puppy's Poo

Bring waste bags to clean up after your dog when you go for a walk outside. I mean, do you want to

step in dog poo? Well, neither do the other guests! Also, if your furkid has an accident in the room, clean it up immediately.

Think About Flea Control

When staying in a pet-friendly hotel, it's no surprise there's going to be a lot of dogs around. You never know who stayed in the room before you or what's lingering in the grass on the grounds. To be safe, consider flea preventative before your trip. I do say this one from experience because, courtesy of a pet-friendly hotel, we had our first case of fleas.

Don't Bring Your Pooch into the Dining Area

In the United States, there are health laws that prohibit dogs from being in areas where food is prepared or served. So, when walking through the hotel, avoid these areas with your furkid. If you want to eat with your pup by your side, some hotels and/or restaurants offer outdoor patio dining. Otherwise, you may want to plan room service or take out and eat in your room. That's actually what I do when I'm on the road. I get to kick off my shoes and relax while my little Diego and Gigi are happily by my side.

Report Any Damage to the Front Desk

If your dog did any damage to the room, bring it to the front desk staff's attention. It's always better to let them know. Maybe they'll charge you for the damage, maybe they won't. But one thing is for sure—if you leave unreported damage they will find it and come after you. On that same note, if you arrive at a room and see any damage, report that as well so you don't become the one responsible for it.

MORE HOTEL ADVICE

Request a Ground Floor Room

Trust me on this one—it will make your late night and early morning potty breaks way easier.

Take a Long Walk Before Entering the Hotel

Before you even enter the hotel, let your dog go to the bathroom and stretch his legs. This will help for a few reasons. First: Letting your dog roam around will allow him to sniff and explore, ultimately helping him acclimate to his new surroundings. Second: If you wind up in a room where other dogs have stayed, he'll likely smell them and want to mark. Luckily, your pup will have just emptied his bladder! Third: A tired dog is more likely to relax once you get inside your room.

Walk Into the Room Before Your Dog

Before slipping the key into your hotel room's door for the first time, I recommend telling your dog to sit. Then, once the door is open, make sure you walk in first. This will set a confident vibe for your dog, letting him know the area is safe.

Walk Around with Your Dog as He Checks Out the Room

Once inside your hotel room, your dog will likely explore. If your pooch is anything like mine, he'll sniff everything from the beds to the bathroom trash can. I always like to walk around with my dogs as they explore so they feel safe and content knowing they aren't alone in a strange place. I also take a peek under the bed, around the other furniture, and inside the trash cans to ensure nothing unsafe was left behind and within their reach.

Bring Toys and Blankets From Home

Once you're in the hotel room, it's always a good idea to offer your dog something familiar. For example, I never enter a hotel room without a few of their favorite toys and blankets. It lets them smell home, which is comforting to your pooch.

CHAPTER 13

Pup-arazzi

As a blogger, I view the world through my camera lens. I spend hours dreaming up creative photo ideas, scouring the web for adorable doggy outfits, and gathering fun props. I carve out entire days for snapping and editing photos of my pups. But, this wasn't always the case.

Back when Diego and Gigi were puppies, I didn't have the same appreciation for great photography. As a result, if I want to look back at their precious puppy days (*which I do, often*), I only have a few dark and grainy iPhone snaps. Don't get me wrong: Smartphones take amazing pics today. But, back then, the quality wasn't as good. And I really wish I had some high-quality puppy pics of them to treasure forever.

Throughout this book, I've shared a lot of important health, training, and lifestyle info. While documenting your dog's journey through photos isn't going to prolong their lifespan or make navigating dog parenthood any easier for you, I still wanted to include a chapter on the topic. I just think capturing memories through photographs is important!

LIGHTS, CAMERA, ACTION: GETTING READY FOR A PUPPY PHOTOSHOOT

As silly as it sounds, I recommend every new dog mom schedule at least one photoshoot with a professional photographer when their furkid is still a puppy. The puppy stage is fleeting, and over before you know it. Even if your puppy isn't fully trained yet, the photographer can capture plenty of great candid shots. But, I promise you'll look back at these keepsake photos for many years to come and they'll immediately put a smile on your face.

Choose Your Style and Create a Must-Have Shot List

What type of photos do you like best? Do you get lost in Instagram accounts that are light, bright, and airy? Do you prefer saturated colors that pop? Or maybe you like darker tones. Do you like candid shots of dogs playing or posed portraits? Full body shots or closeup details?

Spend some time looking at popular dog accounts on social media and create a vision board that you can show to your photographer. This is your time to get creative, dream up the details, and think about what you want out of the shoot.

While you're on Instagram looking for photo inspo, connect with me and my pups @prouddogmomblog!

Find a Photographer

If you already know a professional photographer who you trust and whose work you admire—great. That makes this step easy. But, if not, spend some time Googling local photographers. Look into professionals who specialize in pet photography *(yes, that's a thing!)*. Spend some time on their website, review their portfolio, check reviews, and reach out to request pricing.

When you reach out to photographers, ask them how they work. Do you book a set amount of time? During that set time, are you allowed to change clothes? If so, how many looks can you plan?

Read the Fine Print

Before you book a session with a photographer, make sure to read their contract's fine print and understand their full obligation to you. After the shoot, will they give you a USB or access to an online gallery of all edited photos? Will they hand over watermarked photos with the photographer's name? If so, is there a fee to remove that watermark? Can you post the photos anywhere you want? Get the details clear before you hand over any money and before any pics are snapped!

Location

As you plan for your photoshoot, you'll need to think about backdrops. One of the easiest places to shoot is in your home or backyard. It's where your dog is most comfortable and relaxed, which means his personality is bound to shine. It's also where all your stuff is, making it super convenient. Plus, the show can go on rain or shine!

If you're looking to get outdoors, though, parks, open fields, or dog-friendly lakes and beaches are another great idea.

Glam

Before a photoshoot, have your dog freshly groomed and looking spiffy. This isn't the time to experiment with a new haircut—his regular puppy cut is perfect. If your pup hasn't gone in for a trim yet and you want to capture his fluffiness then at least bathe him and run a comb through his hair.

If you plan on making an appearance in the photos, get your hair and nails done too. If you're a makeup master then you can easily do your own. But, why not go all out and get pampered by a pro makeup artist? After all, this is a special day!

Outfits

Confession: I love matching outfits. Whenever I plan a photoshoot, I organize *my* clothes around *my dogs'* outfits. If you're not the matchy-matchy type, still spend some time thinking of complementary colors (*i.e. teal and pink, royal blue and yellow, sky blue and orange*) and patterns. Avoid anything that clashes or isn't aesthetically pleasing.

If you don't dress your dog up in clothes, focus on accessories. They can wear a themed bandana or eye-popping harness and leash set.

Props Are Your Friend

- Plush toys, treats, and chew sticks are great props if you're looking for interactive puppy photos.
- Celebrate your puppy's gotcha day by making a dog cake (*recipe on page 127*) and capturing his face as he's about to dig in.
- Dogs sitting next to signs featuring a funny or sentimental note are pretty popular.
- Is there anything cuter than a puppy sitting in a basket?

- Dogs sitting next to a bouquet of colorful balloons makes for a fun photo.
- Blow some bubbles near your pup and capture his reaction!
- If your puppy shoot takes place in the fall, you may consider getting a few pumpkins for your puppy to sit near.
- If your puppy shoot takes place in the winter, I only have one question: Do you wanna build a snowman? Your pup would look so cute sitting next to a mini Olaf!
- If your puppy shoot takes place in the summer and you love the beach then perhaps your pooch can sit on a surfboard.

You get the idea. With a little imagination and creativity, the possibilities are endless!

Take a Walk

A very wise person once said: A tired dog is a good dog. Well, I can tell you from experience, that is very true. To help your puppy burn off excess energy and begin his photoshoot relaxed, take him for a walk beforehand.

Bring Treats

I'm not talking about the everyday treats. For your photoshoot, you want to pull out the high-value stuff. Baked liver bites, dehydrated sardines, little bits of boiled chicken, peanut butter bites – whatever your dog goes nuts over. Having high-value treats nearby will encourage your puppy to pay attention and follow instructions.

EXTRA TIP: *Have fun!*

TIPS TO TAKE PAWSOME PUP PICS

Follow the Rule of Thirds

For more dynamic pictures, don't put your dog smack dab in the middle of a photo. Instead, move your subject (*AKA your pup*) slightly off to the side. To follow the rule of thirds, simply imagine a grid, divided evenly into thirds, both horizontally and vertically. This imaginary checkerboard leaves you with nine equal parts. Place your subject at the intersection of those dividing grid lines, or along one of the lines itself. This popular off-center composition is more natural and pleasing to the eye.

Get Down to Your Dog's Level

Often, when pet parents snap photos of their furkids, they grab their camera, hold it near their face or chest, point it down toward their dog, and click. While the photo will, of course, come out cute because it features your dog, we can make it a whole lot better. Instead, get down to your dog's level. That may require you to bend down on your knees or, if you've got a super short dog, lie down on your belly. This offers a more unique viewpoint.

Play Around with Angles

Photographing from your dog's level is great, but it's not the only creative angle! Stand on a chair and try taking aerial shots. If your pup is resting on the back of the couch (*my little guys do this all the time*) then grab your camera, crouch down, and shoot up. Play around with a bunch of different angles until you discover your favorites.

If you're shooting with a smartphone, try turning it upside down, so the camera is at the bottom. Your phone should naturally flip the image—so you won't get an upside-down shot—but it creates a drastic angle difference.

Add Depth

Rather than sitting your pup in front of a blank wall, leaving you without any interesting depth, take a few minutes to think about the foreground, middleground, and background. Adding a little dimension goes a long way!

Go for Natural Light

If you want good photos, you've gotta have good lighting. Keep in mind: Even though light looks white to your eyes, it does have color. If you're shooting inside, the best thing you can do is turn off all your lightbulbs and rely on the natural light pouring in from your windows. If you leave your lights on, depending on your bulbs, you'll get a yellow or blue tint.

Natural light also has color. Early morning and late afternoon sunlight has a warmer tone. Midday light is cooler.

Whenever I'm photographing outdoors, I keep my fingers crossed for cloud coverage. Direct sunlight is harsh and creates hard shadows. Instead, the clouds are like nature's softbox!

Be Mindful of Backlight

Unless you're after a silhouette look, don't shoot toward a window. All that light pouring into the background will leave your dog's face shaded and dark. Instead, position your pup to face the window—or whatever the light source—so the natural light creates the perfect glow on him.

Pick a Focus

If you ask me, focusing on a dog's eyes is pretty powerful. It's as if they're talking through those peepers. When I'm photographing my dogs, I love to get close and focus on either their eyes or their boop-able snout. Whichever feature is your favorite, experiment with different focal points.

Always Edit

Even if you think your photo is gorgeous as is, editing makes a huge difference. There are plenty of Lightroom presets that drastically change the look of your photos within seconds. My favorite presets are called Color Pop (*which lightens, boosts contrast, and bumps up saturation*) and Light and Airy (*which boosts light and softens color*). Experiment with a few to find your favorite look!

4 WAYS TO GET YOUR DOG TO LOOK AT THE CAMERA

Whether you're in the middle of a professional photoshoot or you're the one behind the camera, at some point, you'll likely need your pup to look at the camera lens. In my opinion, there's something awe-worthy about a great pic where the dog is looking directly into the camera. But sometimes holding a dog's gaze during photoshoots isn't as easy as just calling out their name. So here are some dog photography tips that work for me!

Place a Treat Right Above the Camera Lens

Whenever I plan a puppy photoshoot, I load up on healthy treats. First, I get my dogs interested in the bait by letting them smell the snack. Then, I call out a command like Look, Sit, or Down. Directing them to stay, I place the treat above my camera lens. This gives the illusion they're looking right into the camera. After I snap a few shots, I reward my pooches with praise and, of course, the treat!

Hold Their Favorite Toy Above the Camera

Does your dog have a favorite plush toy or ball? Just like with treats, placing a toy near the camera lens is a great way to get your dog's attention. If the toy has a squeaker then go ahead and make it squeak—it may trigger some great facial expressions.

Make a High-Pitched Noise

If, for some reason, my dogs aren't interested in a treat or toy then I try making high-pitched sounds. This usually draws their attention and promotes that adorable doggy head tilt! Just keep making different sounds until your pooch looks your way. *Warning: If you're doing this in a public place, you may get some strange looks from passersby.*

Have Patience

If you've planned a photoshoot at a public place with a lot of action then your canine cutie may be too distracted to focus on you. Figure out what's holding your dog's attention and position yourself carefully. You want to be somewhere between your dog and whatever it is that's catching his attention. He'll look right through you *(and, unintentionally, at the camera)*.

Thank You!

I hope the many tips, tricks, and hacks packed inside this book help you navigate your dog mom journey. The life lessons and experience we gain by having a canine companion is priceless. They truly are incredibly special creatures.

When my mom and I decided to team up and launch our blog–prouddogmom.com–back in 2016, we never imagined we would come this far. Our small passion project turned into a full-time business. Since our beginning days, we've grown to reach millions of people a month on social media, we've opened up a shop filled with fun goodies for dog moms, published a dog treat cookbook called *Proud Dog Chef: Tail-Wagging Good Treat Recipes*, and now we're getting to share this second book, *Becoming a Dog Mom: The Ultimate Guide for New Puppy Parents*.

We want to say a big THANK YOU to our loyal readers, followers, and supporters. None of this would be possible without you!

To Veterinarian Ashley Gray, DVM, thank you for reviewing the veterinary care chapter of this book and for your continued support on social media. You are smart, kind, and stunningly gorgeous – it doesn't get any better than that!

And lastly, a giant thank you goes to my Chihuahua, Diego, my toy poodle, Gigi, and my mom's Chihuahua, Pippa. You've seen their photos sprinkled throughout this book and they are the real inspirations for everything we do at Proud Dog Mom!

For more healthy dog treat recipes, DIY projects, training tips, health advice, and more canine lifestyle inspiration, connect with me on www.instagram.com/prouddogmomblog, www.youtube.com/ prouddogmom, and www.pinterest.com/prouddogmomblog. Plus, head over to www.prouddogmom. com and sign up for our newsletter. Once you become a pack member, you'll be one of the first to know when we share new resources and goodies.

INDEX

www.ingramcontent.com/pod-product-compliance
Lightning Source LLC
Chambersburg PA
CBHW042349030426

42336CB00025B/3425